Exploring the

OREGON TRAIL

Exploring the
OREGON TRAIL

AMERICA'S HISTORIC ROAD TRIP

KAY W. SCOTT *and* DAVID L. SCOTT

Globe
Pequot

Essex, Connecticut

Globe Pequot

An imprint of Globe Pequot, the trade division of
The Rowman & Littlefield Publishing Group, Inc.
4501 Forbes Blvd., Ste. 200
Lanham, MD 20706
www.rowman.com

Distributed by NATIONAL BOOK NETWORK

British Library Cataloguing in Publication Information available

Library of Congress Cataloging-in-Publication Data

Names: Scott, Kay Woelfel, author. | Scott, David Logan, 1942– author.
Title: Exploring the Oregon Trail : America's historic road trip / Kay W. Scott, and David L. Scott.
Description: Essex, Connecticut : Globe Pequot, [2023] | Includes bibliographical references and index. | Summary: "A guidebook featuring photos, maps, interviews, and information about the landmarks, facilities, individuals, activities, and towns along the Oregon Trail, from Missouri to Oregon"— Provided by publisher.
Identifiers: LCCN 2022024781 (print) | LCCN 2022024782 (ebook) | ISBN 9781493066070 (paperback) | ISBN 9781493066087 (epub)
Subjects: LCSH: Oregon National Historic Trail—Guidebooks. | Overland journeys to the Pacific—Guidebooks. | Automobile travel—Oregon National Historic Trail—Guidebooks.
Classification: LCC F597 .S38 2023 (print) | LCC F597 (ebook) | DDC 917.9504—dc23/eng/20220531
LC record available at https://lccn.loc.gov/2022024781
LC ebook record available at https://lccn.loc.gov/2022024782

∞™ The paper used in this publication meets the minimum requirements of American National Standard for Information Sciences—Permanence of Paper for Printed Library Materials, ANSI/NISO Z39.48-1992.

CONTENTS

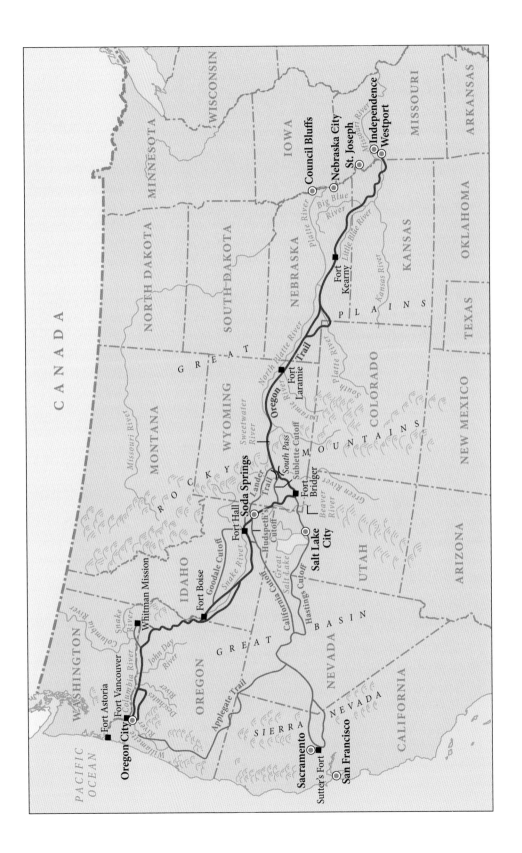

PREFACE

After forty summers of puttering randomly around the United States, mostly in a series of four VW buses, in 2010 we decided to try something different. Following a fiftieth high school reunion in Rushville, Indiana, we headed west to follow the Oregon Trail. From the early pioneers' staging area in Courthouse Square in Independence, Missouri, we drove over 2,000 miles to Oregon City in Oregon's Willamette Valley. During the return east to our home in South Georgia, we followed the Lewis & Clark Trail from the Corps' 1805–1806 winter quarters at Fort Clatsop, Oregon, to St. Louis where the Corps of Discovery had commenced its epic journey in search of a Northwest Passage.

It was a fine summer, with each leg of the trip proving enjoyable and educational. We visited interpretive centers and museums, stopped at dozens of historic landmarks, and met many friendly residents and fellow travelers. The trip proved to be one of the best in our many years of travel. The only downside was Kay declaring upon the return home that we had spent our last night camping in a small tent, which was banished to the attic, where it remains in the event she changes her mind.

Having experienced both the trail of the emigrants' journey to the Northwest and the return route taken by Lewis and Clark, it was easy to declare a winner: The Oregon Trail offered by far the richer travel experience. Little physical evidence remains of Lewis and Clark's journey other than William Clark's inscription of his name on Pompeys Pillar in Montana. Historians know where members of the Corps camped, what they did, and who they met because the entire trip was recorded in great detail in personal journals. Along the Oregon Trail there remain buildings, wagon ruts, graves, and more. We found it easier to imagine pioneer experiences on the Oregon Trail than the Corps of Discovery's experiences searching for a passage to the Pacific.

The 2010 journey following the Oregon Trail was so enjoyable, we repeated the trip 7 years later, during which we described the experience in a weekly travel column for a national newspaper chain.

After acceptance of our 2021 proposal for a book exploring the Oregon Trail, we began planning a third trip nearly identical to our 2017 journey. That is, we would fly to Kansas City, drive the trail in a rental vehicle, and return home on a flight from Portland. This time we spent considerable time studying Oregon Trail history and compiling a list of landmarks we considered important and reachable. (The trail frequently passes through remote locations beyond the reach of most vehicles.) In other places where a landmark was remote and barely reachable, we gave it our best shot.

It is an incredible experience to stand beside a long depression resulting from thousands of wagons being pulled by oxen up a steep incline like that at Nebraska's California Hill. Likewise, standing atop Wyoming's Independence Rock and viewing the zigzag of the Sweetwater River that pioneers were required to cross several times is a sight long remembered. Along the trail are excellent interpretive centers including those at Fort Kearny, Chimney Rock, Scotts Bluff, Fort Laramie, and Casper in Wyoming; Montpelier in Idaho; and Oregon City and, best of all, the National Historic Oregon Trail Interpretive Center outside Baker City in Oregon.

Unlike the Lewis & Clark Trail, along which there is virtually no remaining physical evidence of the Corps of Discovery's journey, numerous sections of the Oregon Trail include ruts, physical structures, graves, and monuments. Imagine the pleasure of strolling a golf course fairway along a lengthy depression made by thousands of pioneer wagons headed across Idaho. Just as impressive is standing in 5-foot-deep ruts in sandstone cut by wagons and livestock traveling through southeast Wyoming. Following the trail and experiencing these historic pioneer footprints sparks the imagination to recall one of the most important mass migrations in our country's history.

A major plus of a road trip along the Oregon Trail is that the journey is mostly through rural America. Except for the beginning in Kansas City and ending in Oregon City, a suburb of Portland, larger towns along the way include Topeka, Casper, Pocatello, Twin Falls, Boise, Pendleton, and The Dalles—pleasant communities that are easily navigated.

Another boon is the lack of crowds. Even at major landmarks such as South Pass, we stood alone at the site where emigrants crossed the Continental Divide. Despite the trail being one of the major factors in the expansion of the United States, many travelers, for whatever reason, fail to consider the Oregon Trail when planning a major road trip. This is their loss.

The two of us have enjoyed five decades of roaming throughout the country while visiting all fifty states. We have driven from our home in Georgia to Alaska and across the entirety of Canada. We have traveled Route 66, the Pacific Coast Highway, and US 1 from South Florida to Maine. None matched the rich experience of our journeys following the Oregon Trail. Tracing the route of America's pioneers who sought a new and better life in the Northwest offers a history lesson for today's travelers. We hope thumbing through the landmarks and images in this book will entice you to plan a trip of your own.

—Kay and David Scott
Valdosta, Georgia

ENHANCING YOUR ROAD TRIP

Should you decide to embark on a road trip following the Oregon Trail, here are some thoughts based on our own experiences during three journeys from Independence to Oregon City. Each trip offered an education that made the following trip even better.

1. **If possible, follow the trail from east to west.** The journey is much more meaningful when trail landmarks are encountered in the order experienced by the pioneers. Starting in Independence and driving through the tallgrass prairie, the short-grass prairie, the Rocky Mountains, and, finally, the Columbia Plateau offers a better sense of what it was like for the pioneers, even though they traveled with a lot less horsepower.

2. **Don't hurry.** At least three weeks are necessary to appreciate most of what this road trip has to offer. In truth, a month or more would be even better. If time is limited, consider splitting the trip in half, perhaps by making an initial trip from Independence, Missouri, to near Rock Springs, Wyoming, with a plan to drive the western segment of the trail to Oregon City later. This would allow you to use the Salt Lake City airport at the end of the first leg and the beginning of the second leg.

3. **Don't miss stopping at museums and interpretive centers along the way.** Start with the National Frontier Trails Museum in Independence and finish with the End of the Oregon Trail Interpretive Center in Oregon City. Between these two bookends are numerous museums and interpretive centers to enrich the journey. Interpretive centers in Casper, Wyoming; Montpelier, Idaho; and Baker City, Oregon, are outstanding. Museums in towns along the way including Topeka, Kansas; North Platte, Nebraska; Kearney, Nebraska; Douglas, Wyoming; Boise, Idaho; and The Dalles, Oregon, are certainly worth a visit. Take time to enjoy these interesting places that some very dedicated and knowledgeable men and women maintain for all of us.

4. **Enhance your knowledge of Oregon Trail history prior to departing home and you will experience a much richer journey.** Learning about the pioneers' fascination with western Nebraska monoliths such as Courthouse Rock and Chimney Rock brings these landmarks to life while driving along the North Platte River. Likewise, a sense of the importance to emigrants of Fort Kearny, Fort Laramie, Fort Bridger, and Fort Hall makes your own visit to these historic sites considerably more rewarding. A short bibliography notes books we found helpful for our own travels along the trail. Read the books by Dary, Mattes, and Unruh before leaving home, and take Franzwa and Haines along for the ride.

Millions of years of erosion by the Sweetwater River in southern Wyoming cut the distinctive V of Devils Gate that fascinated pioneers on the Oregon Trail.

5. **Take time to talk with locals who are proud of their hometowns, museums, stores, and history.** Personal interactions enrich a road trip and sprinkle it with memories. It's rewarding to gain the perspective of the people who live where you are a visitor.

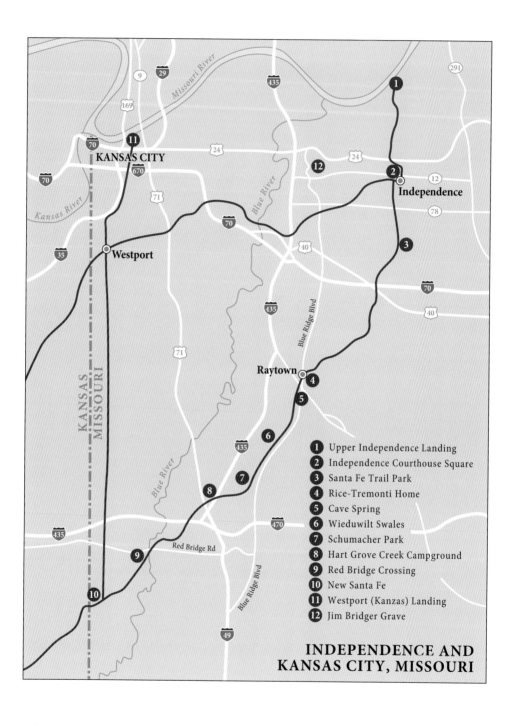

1 Upper Independence Landing
2 Independence Courthouse Square
3 Santa Fe Trail Park
4 Rice-Tremonti Home
5 Cave Spring
6 Wieduwilt Swales
7 Schumacher Park
8 Hart Grove Creek Campground
9 Red Bridge Crossing
10 New Santa Fe
11 Westport (Kanzas) Landing
12 Jim Bridger Grave

INDEPENDENCE AND
KANSAS CITY, MISSOURI

MISSOURI

During the early years of the Oregon Trail, Independence, Missouri, served as ground zero for wagon train departures to the West. As the years passed, emigrants and gold seekers preferred jumping-off locations farther upstream including Westport, Fort Leavenworth, St. Joseph, and Council Bluffs. But during the initial years of migration, Independence Courthouse Square was where the pioneers congregated, acquired supplies, and organized or joined wagon trains for the five- to six-month trip to the Northwest.

Many emigrants arrived at Independence by steamboat from St. Louis, docking 3.5 miles north of town at Upper Independence Landing. Some arrived with only personal items, needing to purchase wagons and oxen for the coming trip. This created a market that resulted in Independence becoming a setting for numerous wagonmakers and blacksmiths. Other emigrants chose to bring along their livestock and disassembled wagons on the steamboats rather than travel overland. Steamboat passage saved nearly 3 weeks of overland travel and reduced wear on both the wagons and livestock. Westport Landing, farther upriver and with better docking, had become the more popular arrival location for steamboats by the mid-1840s.

William Henry Jackson, *Westport Landing* SCBL-(ARCHIVE 19), SCOTTS BLUFF NATIONAL MONUMENT

Emigrants initially departed from Independence by following the route of the old Santa Fe Trail. The trace had long been used by traders to transport goods between the United States and Mexico following the latter country's independence from Spain. The trail from Independence Courthouse Square to the small community of New Santa Fe on Missouri's western border stretched approximately 18 miles. Depending on the weather (rain often resulted in a muddy trail and difficult travel conditions) and the departure time from Courthouse Square, wagon trains stopped for the night at various locations along the trail including the Rice-Tremonti Home, Cave Spring, and Hart Grove Creek before reaching the community of New Santa Fe.

Later in the 1840s the majority of pioneers arriving in Independence chose to travel overland to Westport (now Kansas City) before heading south to meet the Santa Fe Trail a little northeast of New Santa Fe. This would be the last stop in the United States before entering present-day Kansas, which at the time was "Indian country" or "Indian Territory," where the emigrants would become trespassers.

1. Upper Independence Landing

Upper Independence Landing on the Missouri River was the nearest docking location for overland travel to Independence, 3.5 miles distant. Lower Independence Landing at Blue Mills was in the vicinity but not heavily used due to issues with sandbars, frequent muddiness, and a somewhat greater distance from Independence.

In the early 1840s Upper Independence Landing bustled with activity. As passengers disembarked and animals and cargo were unloaded from steamboats, the landing's levee was often a madhouse. Crates and barrels were stacked high; adults scurried around to corral their animals and children; and wagons that had been disassembled for transport were being reassembled. The hike from the levee to the road was steep and often muddy. Cargo frequently had to be carried up the bank to be loaded into the wagons.

Sandbars left by an 1844 flood of the Missouri River rendered Upper Independence Landing less desirable for steamboats, and most arriving captains began choosing the newer Westport, or Kanzas Landing, 2 miles upriver. This was a grim development for Independence merchants, who convinced the town to install a type of rail system from the levy to Independence Square. Pulled by mules, the railcar operation brought about a temporary recovery, but by 1856, in part due to a shifting of the river, Upper Independence Landing was no longer usable.

Today the historic landing site is on private property. An overlook near the intersection of East Kentucky Road and North River Boulevard is about a half mile south of the location of the original landing site. Exhibits at the overlook interpret the three trails pioneers followed west from Independence.

2. Independence Courthouse Square

Independence, Missouri, had only a few hundred citizens when it was founded in 1827 on the western edge of developed territory. As the eastern terminus of the Santa Fe Trail, the small town enjoyed blacksmith shops, wagonmakers, and outfitters to meet the needs of traders. Availability of these businesses made Independence the preferred jumping-off spot for the emigrants who planned to head west to Oregon and California in the early 1840s.

The activities centered on the courthouse square, which was lined with shops. By the mid-1840s at least a dozen blacksmith shops were busy 14 hours a day as thousands of emigrants with wagons, oxen, horses, cattle, and other animals arrived early each spring. Most spent 2 to 3 weeks in the vicinity while they acquired provisions and organized groups of fifty or so wagons in order to travel in greater safety across 2,000 miles of wilderness that at the time was outside the United States.

Some emigrants camped behind buildings that surrounded the square while others preferred to move a mile or two outside Independence, where grass was available for the animals. If oxen were purchased in Independence, time was required to train the teams. Getting ready to head out, the emigrants would gather at **Independence Courthouse Square.**

The courthouse that dominates Independence Square served as the official starting location for emigrants heading west.

A President's Home Where the Oregon Trail Began

Independence, Missouri, not only served as the early demarcation point for pioneers heading to Oregon, it would also be the hometown of **Harry S Truman,** our nation's thirty-third president. The home in which he and his wife, Bess, lived most of their lives is administered by the National Park Service. The site's visitor center is a block north of Courthouse Square, the location where pioneers once gathered in preparation for the trip west. The Truman home is four blocks west and one block north of the courthouse.

Harry Truman was born in a small Missouri town south of Kansas City. He grew up in Independence and married his childhood sweetheart, Elizabeth (Bess) Virginia Wallace, after returning from serving in France during World War I. Other than their years spent at the White House in Washington, D.C., the couple lived in the Independence home of the bride's grandfather for the remainder of their lives.

During Truman's presidency, the house in Independence was referred to as the "Summer White House." Following his presidency the home was frequently surrounded by people seeking a peek at the president, causing the Secret Service to erect a wrought-iron fence to keep the crowds back. Upon returning home from Washington, Truman selected Independence as the site for his presidential library and helped supervise its construction.

Bess Truman's last will left the large Queen Victorian home "to the United States of America to preserve the legacy of her husband and the presidency." Free ranger-guided tours are available. Tickets required for tours can be obtained at the National Park Service visitor center, which offers a 12-minute orientation video about Truman and his life in Independence. For information on days and times of operation, call the Harry S Truman National Historic Site at (816) 254-2720.

Harry Truman's home in Independence, Missouri, is near Courthouse Square, where pioneers gathered before heading west.

Following an 1844 flood that made docking steamboats at Upper Independence Landing more difficult, a new upstream landing was used. Westport Landing shaved several miles off the journey, and, being beyond the mouth of the Blue River, resulted in one less river to cross. By the 1850s, most emigrants were departing from Westport Landing or other locations farther north, and the merchants in Independence had seen the majority of their business vanish.

Today's Independence Courthouse Square continues to present a feel of the past. Not the past of the 1840s, but a feel similar to what many of us now on Social Security may have experienced in our own hometowns. It's an enjoyable place to stroll, and even though the 1840s courthouse has been expanded and renovated several times, the current building is worth exploring. A monument on the west lawn of the courthouse declares, "Here the Oregon Trail Began." It speaks the truth and is a good place for a picture before starting on your own trip to the Willamette Valley.

3. Santa Fe Trail Park

Santa Fe Trail Park is a 45-acre recreational area that includes a quarter mile of historic Oregon, California, and Santa Fe Trail ruts. The Kansas City Park Board acquired the property in 1967 after being informed of the old ruts. The park is at 2900 S. Santa Fe Road in Independence. To view the ruts, follow the entrance drive as it bends to the right and then to the left. The ruts will be on the right in a grove of trees just prior to arriving at the parking area for the tennis courts. The park includes a picnic pavilion and walking trails.

4. The Rice-Tremonti Home

The **Rice-Tremonti Home** sat beside the Santa Fe Trail, 8 miles from Independence. The home's grounds served as a popular camping spot for both Santa Fe traders and emigrants heading to Oregon and California. The family, known for its hospitality, offered food for the pioneers and their livestock. The property had springs for watering the animals and prairie grasses for feeding them.

In 1836 **Archibald Rice** and his family placed a claim on 160 acres they cleared before building a two-story log home and several slave cabins. In 1844 Rice constructed the Gothic Revival frame farmhouse that remains today.

A replica slave cabin near the farmhouse is similar to that in which **"Aunt" Sophia White** moved into in 1850 when her owner married the Rices' son, **Elihu Coffee Rice.** Coffee had become the home's owner when his father died in 1849. "Aunt" Sophia cooked their meals in the hearth of her cabin.

The Rice-Tremonti Home (top) and replica slave cabin (right).

In 1861, at the start of the Civil War, the Rice family and their slaves fled to Texas. They reclaimed the home upon their return to Missouri in 1866. Many homes in the surrounding area had been destroyed during the war, but theirs remained intact. "Aunt" Sophia moved back into her cabin where she lived until just prior to her death in 1896.

Coffee Rice died in 1903 and the house was subsequently owned by two other families, the last being the Tremontis. In 1988 the house became the property of the city of Raytown, where it is maintained and preserved by a nonprofit volunteer organization. The home is at 8801 E. 66th Street in Raytown. Private tours may be arranged by calling (816) 510-8179.

5. Cave Spring

Cave Spring is a 36-acre nature center that once served as a midday rest area and emigrant campground along the Santa Fe, Oregon, and California Trails. The park is less than a mile down the road from the Rice-Tremonti homestead that also served as a campground for many emigrants during their first night on the trail.

The Cave Spring property was settled in 1836 by the Jesse Barnes family and known at the time as the "Barnes Enclosure." Barnes constructed a two-story home and farmed much of his land. The Santa Fe Trail ran beside the property, where the owner allowed emigrants to camp. He also converted the home into an inn and tavern.

Journal entries by emigrants in 1846 noted overnight stays in the home/inn. The property was later owned by the maternal grandfather of President Harry S Truman.

The park has a small cave and a spring, thus the new name. A granite monument was placed at the trail site in 1909 by the Daughters of the American Revolution and the state of Missouri.

In 1975 the Cave Spring Association, a nonprofit group, acquired the land in order to preserve the Santa Fe Trail on the east side of the park. The association manages and maintains the site as a nature center and outdoor education facility with several hiking trails looping through the property. The trails are open to the public from 9 a.m. to sunset. The park is located at 8701 E. Gregory Boulevard in Kansas City. Phone (816) 659-1945 for information.

6. Wieduwilt Swales

Ruts and swales made by wagons, livestock, and people traveling the Oregon Trail are a rare find in a city neighborhood. An exception is a small park where the grass-blanketed depressions are plainly evident at the location where East 85th Street intersects Manchester Avenue in Kansas City. The park is private and maintained by the Cave Spring Association, which permits public access.

Wieduwilt Swales are in a residential area at 85th and Manchester.

On the 85th Street side, about 50 yards from the corner, large swales head south-west. The deep swales resulted from freight and emigrant wagons climbing a hill single file to avoid the large rock formation near the center of the park. A historical marker denotes the site at 7558 E. 85th Street, Kansas City.

7. Schumacher Park

Pioneers in the mid-1800s passed in a westerly direction through the south end of present-day **Schumacher Park.** Although the park no longer offers visible swales or ruts, it does provide visitors with a view of how the prairie would have appeared to the emigrants. Interpretive exhibits have been installed along a sidewalk.

The park is in the southern section of Kansas City. From I-435 take exit 70 east on Bannister Road. Turn left on Hillcrest Road and then right on 93rd Street. The park is on the right.

Schumacher Park has no remaining swales but offers a look at the prairie as experienced by pioneers.

St. Louis: Emigrant Gateway to the West

St. Louis owes its birth to a French fur trading post founded in 1764 near the confluence of the Mississippi and Missouri Rivers. Named for the King of France, the town served as the departure point for the **Lewis and Clark Expedition** and, several decades later, as the gateway for many emigrants who would be heading overland to Oregon and California.

The first steamship arrived here in 1817, setting the stage for St. Louis to become the primary transportation hub for the Mississippi and, later, the Missouri River. In 1821, when traders began traveling overland to Mexico via the Santa Fe Trail, steamships navigated the Missouri as far as **Upper Independence Landing,** about 3 miles north of the town of Independence. This became the location where much of the early overland trade and travel to the West commenced. Traders' merchandise was loaded on steamships at St. Louis for the three-and-a-half-day trip upriver, saving time and 300 miles of overland travel.

When the great westward migration commenced in 1842, many pioneers made their way to St. Louis for steamship passage to Independence, the early overland starting point for the Oregon Trail. As the years passed, emigrants chose jumping-off points farther upstream, but all the while St. Louis remained the main portal through which people and goods made their way up and down the rivers. The population of St. Louis tripled between 1840 and 1850, and then nearly doubled during the subsequent decade. The city was truly the "Gateway to the West," although a large number of travelers apparently decided to make it their permanent home.

In the 1930s the town's civic leaders wanted to commemorate the city's role in the expansion of the United States. A competition for architects was held in 1947–1948 with a design by Eero Saarinen declared the winner. The centerpiece of his plan was a giant stainless steel arch that was eventually completed in1965. The work was initially named Jefferson National Expansion Memorial to honor **President Thomas Jefferson,** who initiated the Louisiana Purchase and organized the Lewis and Clark Expedition. The park later underwent major renovations with a broadening of its scope, and in 2018 was rechristened Gateway Arch National Park.

8. Hart Grove Creek Campground at Marion Park

Wagon trains departing from Independence had to cross the Blue River. With plentiful fish and wild game, the river valley's attractive **Hart Grove Creek** area became a popular camping spot on the night prior to the crossing. The legendary Donner Party camped here in 1846. Exhibits and stone markers define the trail's path along the creek.

Marion Park is located in the "V" where US 71 and I-435 join off Bannister Road. Turn south on Marion Park Drive on the west side of Home Depot, and then west on Hickman Mills Drive. Parking is available in the next block.

9. Red Bridge Crossing of the Blue River

The 235-acre Minor Park, located to the south of Red Bridge Road in Kansas City, offers an 18-hole golf course, tennis courts, a cricket ground, hiking trails, and picnic shelters. Through the middle of the park flows the Blue River, where most wagon trains departing from Independence in the 1840s and 1850s experienced their first river crossing. The park is home to outstanding swales where emigrant wagons were pulled from the river to ascend a hill. **Red Bridge**, a wooden covered bridge, was constructed in 1859 and allowed wagon trains to avoid a ford of the river. The original bridge was later replaced by an attractive metal bridge.

A parking area is at the end of a short drive off Red Bridge Road to the south. The drive, east of Holmes Road and west of the Minor Park North Entrance, isn't named but sports a national park trail sign.

The current Red Bridge was constructed in 1932 to replace an earlier version that itself replaced the original wooden Red Bridge over the Blue River in Minor Park.

The swales are directly south of the parking area. One major and two shallow swales can be seen where pioneer wagons were pulled up the hill after exiting the river. The swales are much easier to discern when the grass is short after a recent mowing.

The Red Bridge is across the railroad tracks in an adjacent section of the park. To access the bridge, drive across the current bridge and turn right onto the park entrance road. Railings on each side of the bridge are decorated with several thousand "love locks," padlocks clasped onto the bridge railing by couples who wish to signify their unbreakable love.

10. New Santa Fe

New Santa Fe in present-day southwest Kansas City was once known as Little Santa Fe, a small community that developed where freight wagons laid over in the 1830s during their travels to markets in Mexico and California. About 10 miles south of Westport and 18 miles from Independence, Little Santa Fe was on the Missouri side of the border and the final town before emigrants exited the United States into Indian Territory. Whiskey was not allowed in Indian Territory, and New Santa Fe was the last place where it could legally be sold. Not surprisingly, the little town was home to several saloons.

The small cemetery is all that remains of New Santa Fe.

Today's travelers find a Kansas City neighborhood where the town once stood. Light swale remnants are visible in privately owned New Santa Fe Cemetery, which we found interesting to explore. The cemetery is home to gravestones from the 1800s along with interpretive information about the Overland Trail. The cemetery is located on West Santa Fe Trail, 0.1 mile east of State Line Road. It sits behind a church across from West 122nd Street.

11. Westport (Kanzas) Landing

By the mid-1840s **Westport Landing** had overtaken Upper Independence Landing as the location where emigrants arriving by steamboat from St. Louis disembarked. The new arrival point was blessed with a large rock ledge at river's edge, making it easier for steamboats to navigate. Emigrants arriving at Westport Landing also benefited from being farther upriver and beyond the Blue River, which emigrants using Upper Independence Landing were required to cross.

The town of Westport, 4 miles from the landing, was near the Missouri state line, which at the time was the western border of the United States. To the west was land that had been given to American Indians relocated in the 1830s from eastern states.

Westport Landing replaced Upper Independence Landing in importance and later grew into today's Kansas City.

As part of the treaty, American Indians were allocated money, some of which was spent in Westport. Thus the town was relatively prosperous prior to becoming the primary departure point for pioneers heading west.

Businesses in town grew to take care of pioneer needs, and by the end of 1846 the economies of Westport and its landing were booming. The population of 300 more than doubled in one year, and the town that sprang up next to the landing was officially named Kanzas. As growth continued through the early 1850s, the name was changed to City of Kansas and, in 1889, Kansas City.

The landing where the emigrants arrived on steamboats is now part of an industrialized area of the city. The Riverfront Heritage Trail is a wide walkway alongside the river accompanied by interpretive signs describing the riverfront's historic past. The old landing site is accessed via a pedestrian bridge at the north terminus of Main Street near the intersection with East 2nd Street.

12. Jim Bridger Grave

In 1868, following decades exploring the West, mountain man, scout, and trapper **Jim Bridger,** suffering various health problems, returned to his home in Westport, Missouri. Bridger had purchased his Westport farm in 1855, but discovered

Jim Bridger's grave is in Mount Washington Cemetery.

Jim Bridger: Mountain Man Extraordinaire

Jim Bridger was 17 years old in 1822 when he headed west for the first time as part of a fur-trapping expedition. At the time he was an excellent shot and skilled at finding his way and surviving in the wilderness. Bridger trapped alone for several years and in 1830 became part owner of a fur company. Not fond of operating a business or staying put, he sold out in 1834 and moved on.

Jim Bridger statue outside the National Frontier Trails Museum in Independence.

In 1843 Bridger and **Louis Vasquez** established a trading post in present-day Wyoming. Facing a declining fur trade, the two planned to take advantage of the overland migration to Oregon. **Fort Bridger** operated for 15 years selling provisions and repairing wagons.

During this same period, Bridger was working as a guide leading wagon trains and expeditions for the US Army. One of his last guiding jobs was leading the Union Pacific survey team during the planning of a route for the transcontinental railroad.

As part of a storied career, Jim Bridger explored a large swath of the Rocky Mountains and beyond and was one of the first white men to see the Great Salt Lake, the Black Hills of Wyoming, and geysers in the Yellowstone area. He accumulated an extensive knowledge of western geography and was said to be able to sketch an accurate map of nearly anywhere he had traveled. He could not read or write but spoke English, French, Spanish, and learned to communicate in several native tongues.

Bridger's private life included three marriages to American Indian women (two of whom died) and eight children. In the early 1850s Bridger purchased a farm in Westport, Missouri, where he built a two-story house. He had planned to retire, but felt the call of the West and returned to the mountains. With failing eyesight he returned to Westport and his family in the late 1860s. Bridger died in 1881 at age 77 and was buried in an unmarked grave in a small cemetery near his home. In 1904 his remains were moved to Mount Washington Cemetery in Independence.

he wasn't yet ready to settle down. It was here in 1881 he died at 77 years of age. Bridger was buried in an unmarked grave in a cemetery near his home.

In 1904 **Major General G. M. Dodge,** one of the US Army officers for whom Bridger scouted, had the former trapper's remains moved to Mount Washington Cemetery in Independence. An impressive memorial erected by the general marks the gravesite.

To visit Jim Bridger's burial site, enter Mount Washington Cemetery at the corner of US 24 (Winner Road) and Brookside Avenue. Take the first left beyond the cemetery office and bear right at the fork just beyond the chapel mausoleum. The large monument is ahead in a triangular grassy area on the left.

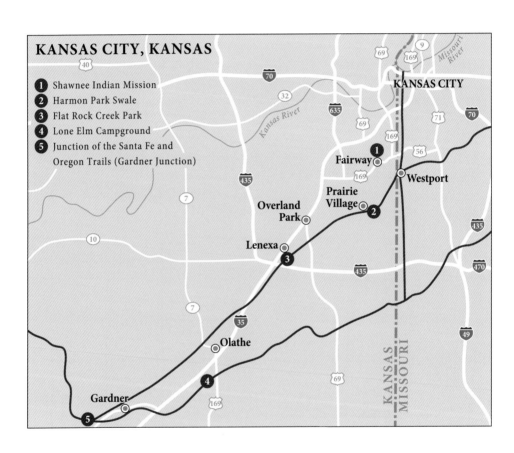

KANSAS CITY, KANSAS

1 Shawnee Indian Mission
2 Harmon Park Swale
3 Flat Rock Creek Park
4 Lone Elm Campground
5 Junction of the Santa Fe and
   Oregon Trails (Gardner Junction)

KANSAS CITY

Fairway **1**

Westport

Prairie
Village

Overland
Park

2

Lenexa

3

Olathe

4

Gardner

5

KANSAS
MISSOURI

Kansas River

Missouri River

KANSAS

Leaving Missouri, the pioneers would travel approximately 170 miles through the northeast corner of present-day Kansas on their way to the Platte River. By 1848 Fort Kearny would be there to assist them. This portion of the trip included some difficult river crossings along a route that offered plentiful water and vegetation for livestock. As the years passed, emigrants increasingly departed Missouri from north of Independence and Westport, in part because of the high incidence of cholera in these towns, but also because river crossings farther north saved travel time. However, in the early years the route that commenced in Independence Courthouse Square offered a relatively pleasant journey through a land that in 1861 would become the country's thirty-fourth state. For today's traveler it is one of the most pleasurable drives, with little traffic, small towns, and some wonderful landmarks of the trail.

The exit from Missouri commenced after a night of camping in Little Santa Fe on Missouri's western border. The sale of alcohol was illegal in Indian Territory, resulting in some excessive drinking during the night in Little Santa Fe.

A dozen miles southwest of Little Santa Fe, Lone Elm Campground was a popular spot to camp on the emigrants' first night after exiting the United States. Not far

William Henry Jackson, *Alcove Springs* SCBL-(ARCHIVE 20), SCOTTS BLUFF NATIONAL MONUMENT

west of Lone Elm the trail to Oregon split from the Santa Fe Trail and headed north and then west past Blue Mound, which must have seemed like a small mountain to the flatlanders. Rolling through present-day Lawrence and then Topeka, where most emigrants crossed the Kansas River, the trail headed northwest along today's US 24 past St. Mary's Mission, a Jesuit school established in 1847 for Potawatomie children.

The emigrants continued northwest to cross the Vermillion River, and then the Big Blue at Independence Crossing near Alcove Spring, one of the most delightful stops along the trail, both during the 1840s and today. The Donner party found itself delayed for several days by high water at Independence Crossing, an unfortunate occurrence that played a part in their late arrival in the Sierras where they encountered an early snowstorm and some unpleasant consequences.

Continuing northwest from the crossing, the wagon trains passed beside Hollenberg Station, a ranch house built in 1857 offering groceries, meals, and rooms, and later, a Pony Express and stage station. At this point the emigrants had to travel only about 8 more miles until they arrived in present-day Nebraska.

1. Shawnee Indian Mission

The 1825 Treaty of St. Louis forced the Shawnee and other eastern tribes from their home territories onto land set aside west of the Missouri River. At the request for a missionary by the chief of the Missouri Shawnees, **Reverend Thomas Johnson**, a Methodist appointed by the missionary society, arrived in present-day Kansas City in 1830 with his new bride.

It was Johnson's idea to build a central school for the children of several tribes, including Shawnee, Kansa, and Delaware. The boarding school opened in 1839 to forcibly assimilate Indigenous children by teaching basic academics, manual arts, and agriculture. At its peak the mission occupied 2,000 acres and sixteen buildings with an average of 200 Indigenous boys and girls, ages 5 to 23, living at the school. The grounds of the **Shawnee Indian Mission** served as a popular campground for emigrants on the Oregon Trail. The mission school closed in 1862 and subsequently found use as a Union Army barracks, dance hall, apartments, and boardinghouse.

The state acquired three buildings in 1927, and today the former mission is a state historic site and National Historic Landmark that occupies 12 of the original 2,000 acres. One of the three brick buildings is open to the public as a museum with a nominal admission fee charged. The East Building houses several exhibits related to the American Indian boarding school, the Johnson family, missionaries, overland trails, "Bogus Legislature," and the Union soldier encampment.

One of the buildings at Shawnee Indian Mission State Historic Site. COURTESY OF SHAWNEE INDIAN MISSION STATE HISTORIC SITE

Shawnee Mission State Historic Site is at 3203 W. 53rd Street in Fairway. Exit north from US 56 onto Mission Road. Take a right on West 53rd, and the mission is on the right. It is open Wednesday through Saturday from 10 a.m. to 4 p.m. Phone (913) 262-0867 for information.

2. Harmon Park Swale

Harmon Park and **Santa Fe Trail Park** sit side by side in the city of Prairie Village at the corner of West 78th Street and Delmar. The location's water tower makes it relatively easy to locate the park. A rock marker with "Harmon Park" and a Santa Fe National Historic Trail logo is to the right of the park entrance.

Inside the park, drive between the tennis courts and the water tower to the end of the parking area near the picnic pavilion. Follow the walkway to the southeast to view an excellent 140-foot-long swale that runs in a northeast–southwest direction. At the end of the walkway is an exhibit with a painting, *Prairie Highway*, by James Hamile, that was commissioned by the city and the National Park Service. The painting depicts a wagon train traveling through the area that is now Harmon Park.

A post marks the location of a swale in Harmon-Santa Fe Trail Park.

3. Flat Rock Creek Park

Flat Rock Creek Park in present-day Lenexa went by several names including Flat Rock Creek, Indian Creek, Indian Creek Campground, and Indian Creek Rendezvous. The crossing was used by emigrants on the Santa Fe Trail and by the military during the Mexican-American and Civil Wars. Land surrounding the creek served as one of the first overnight stops for pioneers departing from Westport Landing.

The 10-acre city park is accessed where Noland Road intersects West 103rd Street. A swimming pool and tennis courts separated by Flat Rock Creek now occupy land that once served as the pioneer campground. The location where the Santa Fe Trail crossed the creek is noted by a sign.

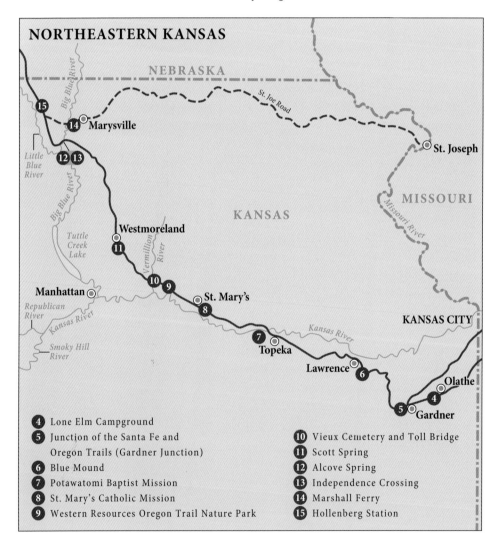

NORTHEASTERN KANSAS

NEBRASKA

St. Joe Road

15

14 Marysville

St. Joseph

Big Blue River

Little Blue River

12 13

MISSOURI

Missouri River

Big Blue River

KANSAS

Westmoreland

Tuttle Creek Lake

11

Vermillion River

10 9

Manhattan

St. Mary's

Republican River

8

Kansas River

KANSAS CITY

Kansas River

Smoky Hill River

7

Topeka

Lawrence

6

Olathe

5 Gardner

4

④ Lone Elm Campground
⑤ Junction of the Santa Fe and Oregon Trails (Gardner Junction)
⑥ Blue Mound
⑦ Potawatomi Baptist Mission
⑧ St. Mary's Catholic Mission
⑨ Western Resources Oregon Trail Nature Park
⑩ Vieux Cemetery and Toll Bridge
⑪ Scott Spring
⑫ Alcove Spring
⑬ Independence Crossing
⑭ Marshall Ferry
⑮ Hollenberg Station

4. Lone Elm Campground

Lone Elm Campground was frequently the first night's resting place for emigrants who departed from Westport. For those leaving from Independence, Lone Elm was generally the location of the second night's stay. Lone Elm was a large campground of about 40 acres blessed with grass and creek water but no trees—with the exception of an elm tree, thus its name. Emigrant journals noted many of the elm's branches had been severed, and comments about the tree continued into 1849. An entry in 1852 noted there was no longer an elm tree, only a large stump.

No wagon ruts or swales remain in what is now Lone Elm Park. However, this former emigrant campground remains an important site because it was the location of the emigrants' first night in Indian Territory. Here groups sometimes circled their wagons, which were then locked together with the front hub of one wagon chained to the rear hub of the next wagon.

Lone Elm Park is south of the city of Olathe, on 167th Street, between US 169 and South Lone Elm Road. A stone marker sits on the southeast corner of 167th Street and South Lone Elm Road. The famed trail campground was located behind the marker.

Little other than a field remains at Lone Elm, a famed gathering place for emigrant wagon trains.

5. Junction of the Santa Fe and Oregon Trails

Emigrants and traders departing Independence and heading west to Santa Fe, Oregon, and California all followed the same trace, the **Santa Fe Trail,** which had been established in the early 1820s. The three trails remained on a single track for approximately 40 miles before separating southwest of present-day Gardner, Kansas. Here the Oregon and California Trails headed west while the Santa Fe Trail continued southwest.

A small roadside park southwest of Gardner, just off US 56 on West 183rd Street, includes a trail marker, a covered interpretive exhibit, and a short nature trail. There are thought to be two possible sites for the actual junction. The first is across the road and behind the first farmhouse to the west on West 183rd Street. This is private property and permission is needed to enter the land. A grove of trees sits behind the farmhouse, and the junction is 0.2 mile back on the east side of the trees.

Another possible location is a mile farther west where the Santa Fe Trail crosses Bull Creek. To view this location, drive west on US 56 past the next intersection where the Santa Fe Trail crossed, and stop about 100 yards after crossing the first small bridge. Walk to the south side of the road. The trail junction followed the crossing of Bull Creek, so look about 250 yards to the south. No actual traces of the trails are in either site, and it is probable both locations were used.

The trails to Santa Fe and Oregon split near this location at Gardner Junction.

The First Emigrant Wagon Train West

Of the many wagon trains heading west in the 1840s, 1850s, and 1860s, the best known is almost certainly that of the ill-fated Donner Party. Among the rest, none is more noted than the **Bidwell-Bartleson Party,** the first emigrant wagon train to travel overland to California. A large portion of the trip followed what would become known as the Oregon Trail.

This interpretive panel is near the location where the Bidwell-Bartleson Party split from the main trail to Oregon.

An economic depression in 1837 and again in 1841, along with upbeat published reports of expeditions to the Northwest, made the Oregon Country appear as an attractive destination. At about the same time, California was being touted by fur traders and others as a land of beauty and opportunity. The chance to start anew influenced many individuals, including Ohio schoolteacher **John Bidwell,** to consider a major change in their lives.

In 1841 Bidwell, with a yearning for adventure, traveled to Missouri. Hearing exciting things about California, he attended a meeting of the Western Emigration Society, an organization that helped prepare emigrants for a westward journey. At the meeting he signed a pledge to join with others at Sapling Grove in today's Overland Park, Kansas, on the ninth of May 1841, to begin a trip west.

The group that gathered selected 54-year-old **John Bartleson** as captain and 21-year-old John Bidwell, who would record daily diary entries, as secretary. None of the members knew the route to California, but the group was fortunate to meet up with **Thomas "Broken Hand" Fitzpatrick,** a famous mountain man, who was guiding **Father Pierre-Jean De Smet** and five other Jesuit missionaries to the Bitterroot Valley of today's Montana.

Fitzpatrick led the group on a path long used by fur traders that would become known as the Oregon Trail. The group reached the Platte River during the first part of June. In early August, near **Soda Springs,** six men decided to return to Missouri on horseback. Fitzpatrick advised the remainder of the party to change their plans and head to Oregon, but one woman and thirty-two men, including Bartleson and Bidwell, chose to continue on to California.

Fitzpatrick's group proceeded to **Fort Hall**, where they traded their wagons and oxen for horses. The Jesuits headed to the Bitterroot Valley, while a guide from the Hudson's Bay Company led the Oregon-bound emigrants north to **Whitman Mission.** From there an American Indian guided the group to The Dalles and, eventually, Oregon City.

Bidwell and Bartleson's California-bound group continued from Soda Springs without a guide or established trail to follow. Along the way they abandoned some wagons and slaughtered oxen for food. They eventually continued on foot, carrying what possessions they could. On November 4, destitute and near starvation, the group reached the ranch of John Marsh. After recovering from the difficult journey, they separated to settle in various California locations.

John Bidwell went on to lead an interesting and prosperous life. While working for John Sutter he discovered gold, acquired a large estate, helped found a university and the town of Chico, and became a California senator and member of the US House of Representatives. His diary describing the trip west was published in 1842 and used as a guide by emigrants.

Many pioneers decided to gain a grand view by climbing to the top of Blue Mound.

6. Blue Mound

About a dozen miles after separating from the Santa Fe Trail and heading north and then west, an early landmark along the Oregon Trail came into view. With nothing other than prairie grass to obscure the pioneers' view, the prominent mile-long bump of **Blue Mound** could be seen from quite a distance.

Blue Mound's summit stood 150 feet above the landscape and was used by frontier explorer **John Fremont** during a 1843 expedition to send a prearranged signal to his Shawnee guides. It was also a popular side trip for pioneers to climb to the summit where they were able to gain a good view of the surrounding prairie.

Tree-covered Blue Mound is approximately 3 miles southeast of Lawrence. From KS 10 exit south on East 1500 Road and drive about 2 miles; the mound will be to the left. Turn east on North 1100 Road, which passes near the south shoulder of the landmark.

7. Potawatomi Baptist Mission

From Blue Mound, the Oregon Trail passed through today's Lawrence. US 40 mostly parallels the trail's route from near the center of Lawrence to the interior of Topeka, where emigrants crossed the Kansas River.

The Indian Removal Act of 1830 had forced the Potawatomi to leave their homeland around the Great Lakes and settle on reserves in present-day Kansas. Missions were built on these reserves with a goal to "civilize" and convert the American Indians to Christianity. The missions received government funding to feed, clothe, and school the children.

American Indian children learned various trades in addition to reading and writing at Potawatomi Baptist Mission.

One of these missions was constructed by Baptists in 1848 near present-day Topeka, and not far from the Oregon Trail. The **Potawatomi Baptist Manual Labor Training School** operated as a boarding school where the children were forcibly assimilated into Anglo culture, learning to read and write English and math. Blacksmithing and farming were taught to the boys, while the girls learned to cook and do needlework. The school operated until the beginning of the Civil War in 1861, when funding was terminated.

An original building from the mission is at 6425 SW 6th Avenue in Topeka. The Kansas Museum of History was constructed on mission property, and the two now reside beside each other. The museum houses exhibits including a covered wagon and a tombstone related to the Oregon Trail.

8. St. Mary's Catholic Mission

After crossing the Kansas River, the pioneers headed northwest to St. Mary's, where the Catholic Church had established its own Indian mission. When the US government forced the Potawatomie to relocate to present-day Kansas, Jesuit missionaries who had been living with the Potawatomie in the East moved with the American Indians to their new land. The missionaries built **St. Mary's Catholic Mission,** where they continued to Christianize the Indigenous people and assimilate their children.

St. Mary's Catholic (Jesuit) Mission once occupied this location in the town of St. Mary's, Kansas.

In the town of St. Mary's, St. Mary's Catholic Mission, built in 1848, became a resting spot for pioneers traveling the Oregon Trail. The Potawatomie, who lived in wigwams around the mission, provided provisions for the emigrants and, farther along the trail, offered ferry service at the Vermillion River.

St. Mary's Academy and College, a private institution not open to the public, is located where the mission building once stood. The institution sits on the north side of US 24 at its intersection with Grand Avenue. A small park with a historical marker is across the street.

9. Western Resources Oregon Trail Nature Park

The **Western Resources Oregon Trail Nature Park** is best known for its large silo painted with a three-part mural, one of which depicts the Oregon Trail. The other panels are devoted to Plains American Indians and Kansas wildlife.

The park has a large picnic shelter with restrooms and three loop walking trails. One trail leads to a hilltop offering excellent views of the surrounding landscape including the route of the historic Oregon Trail that passes beside the park entrance. With a little imagination one can envision prairie schooners traveling alongside the nature park on their way to the Vermillion crossing and **Louis Vieux**'s toll bridge 6 miles ahead.

A gravel road directly overlays the Oregon Trail between Western Resources Oregon Trail Nature Park and Vieux Cemetery.

The nature park is 5.5 miles northwest of St. Mary's. The easiest route is to follow US 24 west to Schoeman Road and turn right. At the end of Schoeman, turn left and follow Oregon Trail Road to the park entrance, which will be on the right. A dusty but more historic route is the gravel road that overlays the old trail. In St. Mary's turn right on 6th, 7th, or 8th Streets, drive three blocks, and turn left on Durink Street. This gravel road leads to the park on your right.

After exploring the nature park, continue northwest on Oregon Trail Road for another 6 dusty miles for a visit to Vieux Family Cemetery and Vieux Crossing of the Vermillion River.

10. Vieux Cemetery and Toll Bridge

Louis Vieux was quite an impressive fellow. Born in Wisconsin in 1809 to a Potawatomi mother and French father, Vieux relocated with his family to Kansas, where in 1857 he acquired a homestead on a hill a short distance east of the Vermillion River. This section of the Vermillion was a natural ford that had been used by such luminaries as **John Fremont, Kit Carson,** and the ill-fated Donner group.

Being a day's travel from St. Mary's Mission, the area was also a popular camping spot for pioneers who had departed from Independence. Although this was a preferred place to ford, the river's steep banks required that wagons be lowered by rope and then raised to the opposite bank. A first-rate negotiator and bright businessman, Vieux constructed a toll bridge that, by some reports, generated several hundred dollars in daily revenues during the busy travel season. Vieux supplemented this income by selling hay and grain to pioneers passing through.

The Vieux family cemetery is near the Vermillion River, where Louis Vieux operated a toll bridge.

Louis Vieux died in 1872 and is buried in the nearby cemetery along with family members including two of his wives. While a number of old gravestones have been replaced, the cemetery is unique and proves a peaceful and interesting place to visit. The area also served as a burial ground for a significant number of pioneers who died here of cholera.

The cemetery and bridge site are about 3 miles east of the community of Louisville. Turn east on Hickory Street, which becomes Oregon Trail Road upon leaving town. A slower but more rewarding route is to follow the Oregon Trail Road west from the **Western Resources Oregon Trail Nature Park** noted in the previous entry.

11. Scott Spring

Water for the pioneers along with adequate vegetation to feed livestock served as magnets for weary travelers searching for a place to rest or camp for the night. A short distance south of Rock Creek and present-day Westmoreland, emigrants frequently chose the attractive area of what is now Oregon Trail Park at **Scott Spring.** In some instances they remained for several days, especially when the creek was high and difficult to ford.

Pioneers' Wagons Were Not for Passengers

Pioneers typically walked rather than rode in their covered wagons. Riding was uncomfortable because, with the exception of the driver's seat, wagons were not equipped with springs. An individual choosing to ride would likely suffer an upset stomach in addition to a very sore rear. But this wasn't the only reason most pioneers walked.

The majority of the wagons on the trail were about half the size of the large Conestoga wagon, which was much too big and heavy for oxen to pull such a long distance. Pioneer wagons were relatively small and could barely hold the necessities and keepsakes emigrants wanted to take along, thus leaving little space for passengers. The smaller wagons that pioneers frequently called "prairie schooners" were about 4 feet wide and from 10 to 12 feet long, with a box 2 to 3 feet deep. Hardwood bows, bent to an inverted U, framed the bonnet, which was doubled-over homespun cotton.

Wagons sported smaller wheels in front than in back to permit slightly sharper turns. Wheels were constructed of hardwood to lessen shrinkage in the hot, dry climate that would be encountered in the West. Hardwood wheels were covered by iron rings, often referred to as tires.

Attached to the side or back of each wagon was a box of repair equipment, a necessity since facilities offering repairs along the trail were few and far between.

Additional items typically attached to the wagon included water barrels, a butter churn, a tar bucket, and a chicken coop complete with chickens that got to ride while the pioneers walked. Tar was used to make a wagon watertight during river crossings.

An empty wagon weighed about 1,300 pounds, and its contents could add up to an additional 3,000 pounds. Four to six oxen or six to ten mules were required to pull a full wagon. Oxen moved relatively slowly but were the choice of most pioneers because of their strength, capacity to withstand fatigue, and ability to survive on grasses and other plants available on the trail. They were also less likely to run off or be stolen.

Smaller front wheels of pioneer wagons permitted sharper turns.

Exhibits interpret life on the trail in Scott Spring Park. The wagon and oxen were welded by artist Earnest White.

Scott Spring is the second of three major springs in present-day Kansas that the pioneers visited during their travel through the state. The spring, located on a steep rock hill a short distance off the west side of KS 99, continues to flow except during the driest of weather. The spring is now on private land with the flow used for watering livestock.

The park itself is on land that was deeded by descendants of the Scott family to the county for 100 years at a cost of $1. Today's travelers owe the descendants their thanks. The property was once under cultivation, and although a pleasant place to explore, no original elements such as ruts or swales remain from the historic trail period. The park does have excellent interpretive boards and an impressive sculpture of oxen pulling a prairie schooner. A 1-mile walking trail is wheelchair-accessible.

Scott Spring Park is on the east side of KS 99 just south of Westmoreland.

12. Alcove Spring

Alcove Spring was and remains today one of the most pleasant stops along the entire length of the Oregon Trail. Pioneers were blessed with a picturesque area of grass, trees, and wildflowers a short distance from a ford of the Big Blue River. Nearby was a rock ledge that hovered about 10 feet above a bowl-shaped pool of cool drinking water. During spring, a wet-weather creek flows over the rock ledge, forming a charming waterfall. A year-round spring flows under the ledge. This area became a preferred campsite of the emigrants. The spring was given its name in 1846 by Edwin Bryant, a member of the ill-fated Donner Party.

Emigrants following the Oregon Trail were not the first people to discover this idyllic spot. American Indians on hunting expeditions had long used the area around the spring as a campground. Later it was used by fur traders and mountain men. **John C. Fremont**'s 1842 expedition camped here, as did **Dr. Marcus Whitman,** who in 1843 accompanied one of the first wagon trains heading west.

Alcove Spring Park is open to the public. While in the area of the spring, look for emigrants' names on the rocks and "Alcove Spring" in the rock at the top of the waterfall, which was carved by a member of the Donner Party. The park offers 5 miles of marked trails through this charming region of Kansas. Swales of the historic pioneer road and a view of the old ford at Independence Crossing are across the road.

To reach Alcove Spring, drive north on US 77 from Blue Rapids past the Georgia-Pacific gypsum mine and take a left onto Sunflower Road, which reaches a dead end at 8th Road. Go right on 8th Road until it meets East River Road. Take another right and continue to the park. A parking area is on the right.

13. Independence Crossing

The Big Blue is a major river pioneers departing from Independence, Missouri, encountered along the trail in present-day Kansas. Those departing from St. Joseph and emigrants following the Council Bluffs Road did not cross here. The ford at the Big Blue, approximately 165 miles from Independence, was appropriately named **Independence Crossing,** apparently after the trail's early departure point. The 359-mile Big Blue, with its headwaters near today's Grand Island, Nebraska, was frequently swollen upon arrival in the early spring, causing wagon trains to delay a day or more until the current subsided.

The consequence of such a delay was especially horrific for the Donner Party, which spent 5 days camping in the area prior to crossing. During their stay, 70-year-old Sarah H. Keyes, who had been ill, passed away and was buried nearby. The lengthy delay at Independence Crossing, followed by a poor choice of routes, resulted in the group becoming trapped by an early snowstorm in the Sierra Nevada. Of the eighty-one people in the party, only forty-five survived.

Directions to Independence Crossing can be found in the description for Alcove Spring, which is across the road from this historic emigrant ford.

14. Marshall Ferry

Most wagon trains departing from Independence crossed the **Big Blue River** at Independence Crossing near Alcove Spring. Emigrants leaving from St. Joseph, Missouri, crossed the river about 6 miles north of Independence Crossing near present-day Marysville.

In 1852 entrepreneur **Frank Marshall** moved here from Missouri for the purpose of establishing a rope ferry on the Big Blue. He enjoyed a brisk business, and emigrants sometimes camped for days waiting their turn to cross despite the hefty charge of $5 per wagon and 25 cents per head of livestock. Marshall operated the ferry until 1864 when a bridge was constructed over the river.

A full-size replica of the rope ferry constructed with sawed logs and square nails is near the crossing site in Historic Trails Park on the west edge of Marysville. Several nearby plaques offer a history of the ferry and the trails that crossed near here. Marysville is also home to a Pony Express museum.

Approaching Marysville from the south on US 77 (10th Street), watch for a Historic Trails Park sign that points toward the right. Turn right (east) on the dirt road, drive for 1.4 miles (passing under US 77), and follow a bend to the north. A side road to the west just prior to another underpass leads to Historic Trails Park.

A rope ferry on the Big Blue River was established near Marysville by Frank Marshall in 1852.

15. Hollenberg Station

German immigrant couple **Gerat and Sophia Hollenberg** in 1858 built a one-room cabin along the Oregon/California Trail near present-day Hanover, Kansas, that was subsequently expanded as the couple entered the hospitality business. Hollenberg, an astute businessman, selected the site because it had creek water and was located near the junction of the Independence and St. Joe Roads. The trail beside **Hollenberg Station** was used by travelers headed to California, emigrants traveling to Oregon, and freight wagons carrying goods to western forts.

The initial one-room cabin was expanded on the east and west sides to accommodate six rooms, four of which served as the family's living space, one devoted to a mercantile store, and another becoming a tavern. The Hollenbergs rented overnight quarters in the attic and served meals to travelers. The property also included a blacksmith shop and large barn.

Hollenberg's facility became a home station for the Pony Express, which operated from April 1860 to October 1861. Home stations housed and fed riders in addition

Hollenberg Station sits beside the Oregon Trail and is thought to be the only remaining Pony Express station in its original location.

William Henry Jackson: The Trail's Artist

William Henry Jackson is noted for many achievements including his famed paintings depicting life on the Oregon Trail. The largest single collection of these paintings is held by the Oregon Trail Museum at Scotts Bluff National Monument in Gering, Nebraska.

Jackson was born in 1843 in Keeseville, New York, to a mother who was a watercolor artist. She taught her son to draw and paint at a young age. As a teenager he held jobs in photography studios and at age 19 served one year as a Union soldier during the Civil War. Upon discharge he returned to the photography studio, where he learned to take and develop photographs.

Jackson decided to head west in 1866 following a broken engagement. In Nebraska City he signed on as bullwhacker for a freight caravan headed to the mines in Montana. Inexperienced in the ways of the West, he learned to round up, yoke, and lead twelve oxen. Splitting from the caravan near South Pass in present-day Wyoming, the future artist headed to California. Along the way he maintained a journal, took photographs, and drew numerous sketches he would later use for painting his famed watercolors.

Returning to Nebraska in 1867, Jackson and his brothers opened a photography studio in Omaha. Excellent photographs taken during his western trip demonstrated Jackson's skill with a camera and helped

Artist William Henry Jackson sits beside his painting of Independence Rock. SCBL-2643, SCOTTS BLUFF NATIONAL MONUMENT

him become the official photographer for the US Geological & Geographical Survey of the Territories for 8 years beginning in 1870. During this period he took the first photographs of the Yellowstone area—images that brought acclaim from the public. The images influenced members of Congress in 1872 to make Yellowstone the nation's first national park. Mount Jackson in the Gallatin Range of Yellowstone National Park was named in his honor.

Following his departure from government, Jackson continued in the photography business until retiring in 1924 at the age of 81. This allowed time for the artist to begin painting, both in oils and watercolors, a practice he continued until his death in 1942 at the age of 99.

to serving as locations for a change of horses. The majority of the Pony Express's nearly 200 stations were "swing" or "relay" stations that provided only a change of horses. Hollenberg Station is generally considered to be the only existing Pony Express station remaining at its original location.

Completion of the transcontinental telegraph doomed the debt-heavy Pony Express, and traffic to California and Oregon trailed off as travelers chose to depart from farther upstream on the Missouri. The change caused Gerat and his wife to concentrate on farming, but in the late 1860s the Hollenbergs departed their rural home and moved to nearby Hanover, a town they founded.

The home and 7 acres were purchased by the state of Kansas prior to the outbreak of World War II. The Kansas Historical Society assumed oversight of the station and acquired an additional 40 acres. The original building was extensively renovated in the early 1990s and includes period furnishings. A nearby visitor center offers exhibits related to the Oregon Trail, Pony Express, and more, along with a small theater.

From US 36, turn north on KS 148 and drive 4 miles to Hanover. Turn east on KS 243 and drive 1 mile to the historic building.

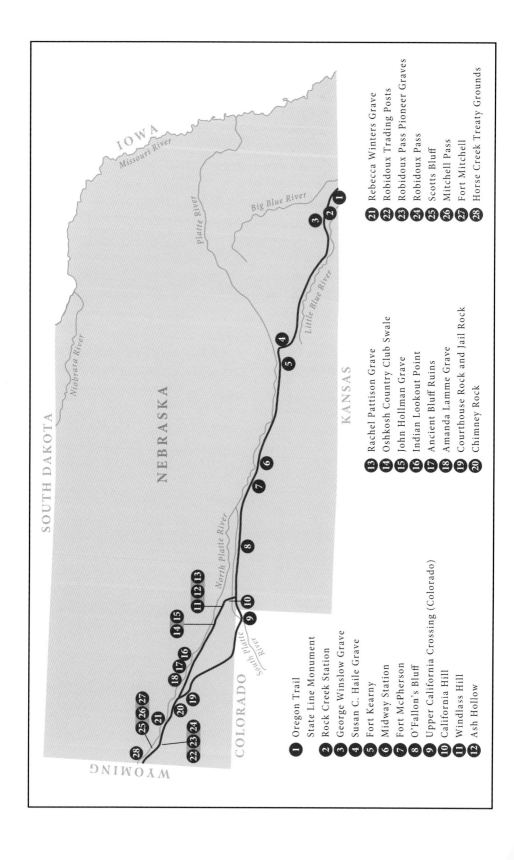

IOWA

Missouri River

Platte River

Big Blue River

Little Blue River

Niobrara River

SOUTH DAKOTA

NEBRASKA

KANSAS

North Platte River

South Platte River

COLORADO

WYOMING

1   Oregon Trail
    State Line Monument
2   Rock Creek Station
3   George Winslow Grave
4   Susan C. Haile Grave
5   Fort Kearny
6   Midway Station
7   Fort McPherson
8   O'Fallon's Bluff
9   Upper California Crossing (Colorado)
10   California Hill
11   Windlass Hill
12   Ash Hollow

13   Rachel Pattison Grave
14   Oshkosh Country Club Swale
15   John Hollman Grave
16   Indian Lookout Point
17   Ancient Bluff Ruins
18   Amanda Lamme Grave
19   Courthouse Rock and Jail Rock
20   Chimney Rock

21   Rebecca Winters Grave
22   Robidoux Trading Posts
23   Robidoux Pass Pioneer Graves
24   Robidoux Pass
25   Scotts Bluff
26   Mitchell Pass
27   Fort Mitchell
28   Horse Creek Treaty Grounds

NEBRASKA

The Oregon Trail crosses from Kansas into the southeastern portion of Nebraska where pioneers followed the eastern bank of the Little Blue River in a northwesterly direction toward the Platte River Valley. In 1848 a new Fort Kearny was constructed a short distance west of where the old trail reached the Platte River. The fort had been relocated to offer better protection for the emigrants, who were able to purchase provisions and enjoy their first touch of civilization. At this point they had traveled nearly 300 miles over relatively easy terrain that had offered plentiful water, grass, and wood.

Upon reaching the Platte River, the main trail from Independence was joined by a trail from Nebraska City, site of the original Fort Kearny. The combined track then headed west along the south side of the river paralleling a trail on the north bank used by emigrants who had departed from Council Bluffs and points north. The combined trails along the Platte comprised what became known as the Great Platte River Road, along which pioneers would gain over 2,000 feet in elevation during 300 miles of travel to reach Fort Laramie. This section of the trail had its share of hardships including summer thunderstorms and sandhills that strained draft animals pulling the loaded wagons, but it was relatively flat with adequate water and grass. More difficult terrain would be encountered farther west near Scotts Bluff.

William Henry Jackson, *Fort Mitchell* SCBL-(ARCHIVE 28), SCOTTS BLUFF NATIONAL MONUMENT

The South and North Platte Rivers, both of which have their headwaters in Colorado, merge to form the Platte just east of today's town of North Platte. Depending on the river's current, emigrants sometimes chose to cross near here and follow the north bank of the North Platte. Most continued along the south bank of the South Platte to cross farther upstream. A major crossing point was west of present-day Brule at the Lower, or Old California Crossing. In later years most trail traffic went farther upstream and crossed at the Upper California Crossing near Julesburg. A short distance northwest of the lower crossing, emigrants encountered their first major ascent at what became known as California Hill. The trail then followed an 18-mile ridge before a sharp descent into delightful Ash Hollow, an oasis with spring water, grass for livestock, trees for firewood, and, on occasion, American Indians.

After resting in Ash Hollow, sometimes for several days, the pioneers veered west out of the hollow to follow the south bank of the North Platte River. Along this stretch that today is sometimes called Nebraska's Monument Valley, the travelers were fascinated with magnificent natural monoliths including Jail Rock, Courthouse Rock, and Chimney Rock, the latter being the most noted trail landmark in pioneer journals. West of Chimney Rock great bluffs blocked travel along the river, requiring a detour to the south before returning to the North Platte. Some difficult stretches remained along the trail to Fort Laramie, but these were merely an introduction to the hardships that lay before them.

1. Oregon Trail State Line Monument

This impressive monument stands near where the Oregon Trail crossed from Kansas into Nebraska.

A large, triangular stone monument marks the approximate location where the Oregon Trail crossed from present-day Kansas into today's Nebraska. Erected in 1913 by the Daughters of the American Revolution, the monument salutes emigrants who passed through on their way to Fort Kearny. The monument sits at the meeting point of three counties, each of which has its name inscribed on one of the sides. Unfortunately, the lengthier inscriptions have eroded and are difficult to read.

Driving north on KS 148 or south on NE 112 (the same road), turn west on State Line Road and drive 2.8 miles on a paved road that turns to gravel. The monument is on the right at the intersection of West Stateline Road and SW 142nd Road.

2. Rock Creek Station

Rock Creek Station was established in 1857 as a road ranch on the west side of Rock Creek, a somewhat difficult crossing for the pioneers and freight wagons headed to Fort Kearny. Perhaps best described as a scaled-down version of a Jiffy Mart, the road ranch sold supplies including hay and grain to wagon traffic traveling along the main route of the Oregon Trail.

The original owner sold the facility in 1859 to **David McCanles,** who expanded the operation on the east side of the creek by digging a well and constructing additional buildings that became known as the East Ranch. He also built a toll bridge over the creek. McCanles subsequently leased the East Ranch to the Russell, Waddell, and Majors Company, owner of the Pony Express and Overland Stage Company, which used the ranch as a stop for both operations.

Rock Creek Station is perhaps best known as the location where **Wild Bill Hickok** first made a name for himself as a gunfighter. Accounts of the event vary depending on the source, but Hickok is said by some to have shot and killed two individuals, including the East Ranch owner who arrived one day to collect past-due lease payments. Found not guilty following a plea of self-defense, Hickok went on to gain fame as a scout, lawman, and gunfighter before being shot and killed during a poker game in Deadwood, South Dakota.

Looking west from East Ranch toward the toll bridge at Rock Creek Station

Wild Bill Hickok's Shoot-out at Rock Creek Station

Wild Bill Hickok brought a bit of renown to Rock Creek Station with a shoot-out that proved the opening chapter in a series of confrontations that made him one of the West's best-known gunfighters. While details are somewhat fuzzy, Hickok may have shot and killed the owner of Rock Creek Station, where he had taken up employment.

Wild Bill Hickok established his reputation at Rock Creek Station. PUBLIC DOMAIN

James Butler Hickok was born in Illinois on May 27, 1837. As a young boy he assisted his abolitionist parents operate a station of the Underground Railroad. In his late teens, following his father's death, he headed west to Kansas where he drove a stagecoach, became a peace officer, and made the acquaintance of a young Bill Cody, who later became known as Buffalo Bill.

In the spring of 1861 Hickok was hired as a stock tender at Rock Creek Station. He and former owner David McCanles had engaged in some harsh words, and when McCanles later visited East Ranch to collect overdue installment payments, a shoot-out ensued. According to one version, Hickok shot and killed the former owner and one of the owner's friends who, hearing gunfire, rushed to help. Another of McCanles's friends who accompanied him to the ranch was killed by an associate of Hickok. Alternate versions of what became known as the "McCanles Massacre" emerged over the years as Hickok's reputation as a gunfighter grew. Hickok was judged not guilty of the Rock Creek Station murder after pleading self-defense.

Following the short but eventful stint at Rock Creek Station, Hickok joined the US Army, where he became friends with General George Armstrong Custer. He was subsequently elected sheriff of Ellis County, Kansas, appointed city marshal in Abilene, Kansas, and assembled an unsuccessful Wild West show. Excessive drinking and gambling proved too much for even Wild Bill when he was shot and killed during a poker game in a Deadwood saloon. His last poker hand—a pair of aces and a pair of eights—became known as the "dead man's hand."

Traffic along the trail began declining in the latter 1860s when rail travel offered faster and more comfortable service. The abandoned facility was acquired by the state of Nebraska, which in 1980 commenced development of a state historical park. A corral and several ranch buildings including a bunkhouse, cabins, and the Pony Express barn have been reconstructed and are open to visitors. The park visitor center has exhibits plus a small theater that shows a 10-minute film. Exceptional eroded trail ruts resulting from thousands of wagons ascending a rise from Rock Creek are a short distance west of the visitor center. A picnic area is near the visitor center, and a developed campground is in adjacent Rock Creek Station State Recreation Area.

Rock Creek Station State Historical Park is an especially interesting and enjoyable stop. Allow several hours to view exhibits in the visitor center, stroll alongside the historic wagon ruts, and explore the reconstructed buildings and toll bridge.

The park is 9 miles southeast of Fairbury. Follow the road signs from NE 15 in Fairbury to the PWF Road, or from US 136 turn south at Jansen, then follow the road signs to the park. The park is open year-round, although the visitor center operates only from mid-April through mid-October. A Nebraska state park entrance permit is required, and a nominal fee is charged for viewing exhibits in the visitor center. Phone (402) 729-5777 for information.

3. George Winslow Grave

Despite the large number of deaths that occurred on the trails, a limited number of graves with stone markers survived. The scarcity of graves is in part due to many of the dead being buried beneath the trail and without a marker in an effort to hide the bodies from animals. One of a limited number of graves with a stone marker is that of 25-year-old **George Winslow.**

Winslow was born in New York and later moved with his family to Massachusetts. He was married in 1845 and had two sons when word of the

George Winslow's original gravestone is embedded in a replacement marker.

California gold strike reached Massachusetts. He joined the Boston and Newton Joint Stock Association that was formed to guide an expedition to California. George Winslow became ill and died of cholera several days later while traveling in present-day Nebraska, where he was buried beneath a stone marker.

In 1912, Winslow's sons had the original marker embedded in a granite obelisk. The later monument includes a bronze tablet with the following inscription: "In Memory of George Winslow who died on this great highway June 8, 1849 and was buried here by his comrades, of the Boston and Newton Joint Stock Association. This tablet is affectionately placed by his sons, George Edward and Orin Henry Winslow." The original stone marker reads: "George Winslow. Newton, Ms. AE25."

The gravesite is located about 5 miles north of Fairbury. From Fairbury drive north on NE 15 and turn west on 716th Road. Continue beyond the first crossroad of 567th Avenue for about 0.4 mile to the first farm gate on the right. You should be able to view the top of the obelisk from the road. The grave is on private property, but the owner is kind enough to offer access to the public. If the gate is closed, walk to the gravesite (be sure to close the gate as there may be livestock in the field). If the gate is open, you may drive to the site. Two excellent swales are evident on the walk to the grave.

4. Susan C. Haile Grave

Susan Haile was one of many pioneers who died of cholera, a bacterial disease that remained prevalent along the Oregon Trail into the 1850s. Susan Haile's grave is especially interesting because it has had at least three grave markers and is accompanied by a story of her life.

Susan Haile's gravestone, located on a lonely Nebraska hill.

Susan C. Seawell was born in Cape Girardeau County, Missouri, in 1817. Married in 1836, she and husband Richard Haile had six children when Richard departed for California during the 1849 gold rush. After mining for about a year, he decided to move his family to California. Returning to Missouri in 1851, they sold their property the following year and headed to California. Traveling with them were Susan's brother and his family, her unmarried sister, and one hundred head of cattle. Her children ranged in age from 3 to 14 years old. There is no record of their journey, only the fact that she died on June 2, 1852.

Where America's Homesteaders Are Honored

Today's travelers following the Oregon Trail between Topeka, Kansas, and Kearney, Nebraska, can take advantage of an interesting side trip. **Homestead National Historical Park**, a few miles west of Beatrice, Nebraska, commemorates and interprets the Homestead Act of 1862 that offered free land to homesteaders. The historical park is on the claim of Daniel Freeman, who in 1863 filed one of the first claims made under the act. The park's 160-acre parking lot represents the size of the land grant.

The legislation resulted in transferring 270 million acres in thirty states from the federal government to individuals. This represented 10 percent of the country's land area distributed out of the public domain into private ownership. The Homestead Act was repealed in 1976, with an exception for homesteading in Alaska, and that was terminated a decade later.

The park's unusual prow-shaped Heritage Center offers a 23-minute film plus numerous educational exhibits with insights about the people, equipment, and living conditions associated with homesteading. Outside, a small homestead cabin illustrates the crowded living conditions that existed for many families that homesteaded. The separate Education Center is devoted to living history demonstrations and includes a museum of tools and farm machinery.

The historical park is in southeastern Nebraska, 4 miles west of Beatrice on NE 4 and approximately 30 minutes northeast of Rock Creek Station State Historical Park. Call (402) 223-3514 for information.

Metal outlines of each state included in the Homestead Act are mounted along the wall leading to the visitor center at Homestead National Historical Park.

The story related through the years is that Richard placed a temporary marker on Susan's grave, left his children in the care of their aunt, and returned to "civilization" with his horses to acquire a marble headstone. Selling his horses to pay for the engraved headstone, he acquired a wheelbarrow and set out on foot, pushing his wife's headstone before him. After placing the marble marker on her grave, he joined another wagon train as a hired hand and worked his way to California ,where he joined his children.

Susan's last name has experienced different spellings including Haile, Hail, and Hale; plus having a middle initial changed from C. to O. The confusion is likely due to her marker being replaced at least twice.

The plot of land that includes Susan's grave was purchased in 1958 and donated to Adams County. The Federated Women's Club of Kenesaw, the Adams County Historical Society, and other people in the area have cared for the grave.

The gravesite is northwest of Kenesaw. From US 6/34 drive west to Spur 1A and turn north toward Kenesaw. Entering town, watch for Pine Street and turn left (west). Drive 1.5 miles to Winchester Avenue and turn right. Drive 3 miles to 70th Street and turn left. Drive approximately 1.5 miles to a small pullout on the right. The grave is about 50 yards to the right.

5. Fort Kearny

Fort Kearny was the first in a series of forts built to assist and protect emigrants traveling along the Oregon-California Trail. The initial Fort Kearny, constructed in 1847 as a log blockhouse near present-day Nebraska City, was short-lived due to poor location selection that placed it near the beginning of the trail. Ordered by army officials to find a location along the Platte River, construction commenced in the spring of the following year on a second Fort Kearny (initially named Fort Childs) near the south bank of the Platte and a little less than 200 miles west of the original fort. The location near the head of Grand Island was at a junction of several trails that joined to form the Great Platte River Road leading west to Fort Laramie. The site offered a limited amount of timber that could be harvested from the island, a rarity in a river valley that was bare of trees.

Like most western forts, Fort Kearny was primarily designed to house soldiers and, as a result, was built without the protection of a stockade. In its early life it was primarily a series of sod buildings surrounding a parade ground. Facilities improved over the years, but most travelers passing through, while pleased to find a link to the civilization they left behind, seemed unimpressed with the fort's appearance. Travelers frequently stopped to conduct business with the fort sutler, a civilian who bought and sold provisions. Emigrants often required a blacksmith's assistance for

A replica sod blacksmith shop is open to visitors at Fort Kearny State Historical Park.

problems with wagon wheels or the shoeing of livestock. Others dropped off letters to be mailed back home.

Declining traffic on the trail, the 1868 signing of an Indian treaty, and progress in building the transcontinental railroad sealed Fort Kearny's destiny. Abandoned in 1871, the land was transferred to the Department of the Interior and offered to home-steaders. Local citizens raised funds and in 1929 purchased 40 acres that included the old parade ground. The land was offered to the state, which in 1960 made it a state historical park.

Nothing of the original fort remains. The state has reconstructed the sod black-smith shop filled with tools and other period artifacts. The 1864 fort stockade and the powder magazine have also been rebuilt. Other buildings that have been lost over time are outlined with stakes. A visitor center offers artifacts that tell the story of the fort's history. A Nebraska state park entry permit is required, and a nominal fee is charged for entrance to the visitor center. The visitor center and buildings are open from May 1 through September 30. Phone (308) 865-5305 for information.

From I-80, exit south on NE 44. Drive about 2 miles, crossing the Platte River, and turn east on NE 50A. Fort Kearny State Historical Park is about 4 more miles, on the north side of the road.

6. Midway Station

Midway Station's 1969 nomination form for inclusion on the National Register of Historic Places states the structure is Nebraska's most important existing building to service traffic along the old Overland Trail. This makes it pretty special, especially considering the building remains at its original location. We can thank the owners of the ranch where it is located for taking care of an important part of America's history.

The station's name is thought to derive from its location midway between Atchinson and Denver. It is generally believed Midway Station was constructed in 1859 by the Levenworth & Pikes Peak Express Company to link the Missouri River with Denver and Salt Lake City. As such, it was one of fifteen stage and mail stations constructed across Nebraska. The stations were acquired the following year by Pony Express owners Russell, Majors, and Waddell. Midway Station continued to serve as a stage and supply station into the late 1860s due to its location on the most heavily trafficked segment of the Overland Trail.

The one-story building was constructed using large, hand-hewn cedar logs. The original section built in 1859 received an addition the following year when it became a Pony Express Home Station, which housed riders and cared for horses. The

Midway Station is beside the Oregon Trail and thought to be one of fifteen mail and stage stations constructed in 1859.

original dirt floor was eventually improved with wood, and later with cement. Grout has been substituted for the mud that was initially used to seal the logs.

Midway Station is a short drive southeast of Gothenburg. Exit I-80 south onto NE 47 and drive 1.8 miles to CR 764. Turn east and drive 1 mile to the station, situated among an impressive agricultural complex with several large silos. The old station is protected by a large metal building with an open front.

7. Fort McPherson

Fort McPherson was established in 1863 following an increase in hostilities with and among American Indians. Known initially as Cantonment McKean and later, Fort Cottonwood, the name was officially changed in 1866 to honor **James McPherson,** a Union general killed during the Civil War. Located on the Oregon Trail between Fort Kearny and Fort Laramie, military personnel stationed at the fort were charged with offering protection to travelers on the trail, nearby settlements, and workers involved in construction of the transcontinental railroad, along with security of the transcontinental telegraph line.

Numerous military campaigns were carried out by the fort's soldiers, who included William "Buffalo Bill" Cody and Lieutenant Colonel George Armstrong Custer. Activities included escorting wagon trains and stagecoaches and hunting and attacking American Indians who were thought to have caused trouble. With a decline in American

A soldier's statue marks the former location of the flagstaff at Fort McPherson.

Indian conflicts, the fort was abandoned by the military in 1880, after which the buildings were auctioned. Nothing of the fort remains, although a monument about 1 mile southeast of the cemetery marks the location of the fort's flagstaff.

A national cemetery on fort grounds was established in 1873 as a burial ground for the remains of soldiers at remote areas of the frontier. The 20-acre cemetery is enclosed by wrought-iron fencing and includes the superintendent's lodge that was constructed in 1876. Over 3,700 interments at the cemetery include four recipients of

This large monument at Fort McPherson National Cemetery honors the soldiers who were killed in the 1854 Grattan Massacre near Fort Laramie.

the Medal of Honor, sixty-three buffalo soldiers who served in the Indian Wars, and twenty-eight soldiers who were killed in an 1854 battle near Fort Laramie. The latter encounter, often termed the **Grattan Massacre,** is considered the opening engagement in a generation-long conflict with the Sioux.

The national cemetery is approximately 4 miles south of Maxwell, via NE 56A. From I-80 take exit 190 and head south. The grounds of the old fort are farther down the road on private property. A parking area is available for those who wish to view the monument marking the location of the Fort McPherson flagstaff.

8. O'Fallon's Bluff

Approximately 25 miles west of the confluence of the South and North Platte Rivers, a stretch of sandstone hills called **O'Fallon's Bluff** once butted up against the south bank of the South Platte. The blockage required Oregon Trail wagon trains to temporarily loop south away from the river and travel over the bluffs. The impediment to pioneer travel is somewhat difficult to visualize today due to a large swath of bluffs being cut away during construction of I-80. Fortunately, swales left by thousands of wagons crossing the hills remain visible for today's travelers.

The Platte River, which served as a superhighway for emigrants heading west.

The history here is somewhat hazy although it is likely the bluff was named for Kentucky-born **Benjamin O'Fallon,** who served as an Indian agent in the 1820s prior to becoming a fur trader. It was reported that during this latter period he lived for a time in one of the bluff's caves. Beginning in the late 1850s, the area served as home to a trading post, stage station, post office, and Pony Express station. O'Fallon's Bluff was frequently noted in pioneer letters and diaries. During the early years of the trail, one of the first fords of the river was east of the bluff.

The section of land containing Oregon Trail swales is now part of a rest stop along the eastbound lane of I-80 between exits 158 and 164. Westbound travelers should use exit 158 to gain access to the eastbound lane. Exit 164 can then be used to return to the westbound lane. The area of visible swales is a short walk along a paved path from the rest stop parking area. Parallel strips of brick pavers and iron hoops representing wagon wheels guide visitors along the trail. Information panels offer details about the trail and bluff.

9. Upper California Crossing (Colorado)

Many of the historic trails started as American Indian paths. In 1856 a soldier discovered one of these passageways that followed the South Platte River into present-day Colorado before crossing to the north bank near today's town of Ovid. Here the river was wide and relatively calm, making it less dangerous to ford. The US Army and freighters made this a popular crossing, as did the Pony Express.

The town of Julesburg started with the trading post of Jules Beni at the Upper California Crossing.

After crossing here, wagons headed northwest toward Courthouse Rock to join the main trail east of Chimney Rock. This route missed the pleasures of a visit to Ash Hollow, but avoided the struggle to climb California Hill and the danger of descending steep Windlass Hill, which confronted wagon trains using the popular crossing 20 miles downstream near today's Brule, Nebraska. The new ford soon became known as "**Upper California Crossing**" while the earlier ford would be called the "Old," or "Lower California Crossing."

As traffic using the upper crossing increased, **Jules Beni** established a nearby trading post around 1858. With the discovery of gold near Pikes Peak in 1859, traffic picked up and Beni added a warehouse, stable, and blacksmith shop to his trading post. Soon pioneers began settling and opening businesses in the area that became a stop for the Overland Stage and the Pony Express. The community would become known as **Julesburg.**

In 1865 Julesburg was burned during an American Indian raid. The town's present location is actually Julesburg IV. Julesburg II and III were established when the Union Pacific railway stations moved.

Markers on CR 28 indicate the original site of Julesburg is 1,235 feet directly north, an area that is now private property. The Upper California Crossing would have been just beyond that point at the South Platte River. To reach CR 28, follow

I-76 into Colorado and take exit 180. Exit to the north and take the first road to the west (left); that is CR 28. Drive approximately 6.5 miles past the Colorado Visitor Center. Interpretive markers are on the north side of the road.

10. California Hill

Having gained a little over 1,000 feet in elevation during 175 miles of travel heading westward from Fort Kearny along the Platte River Valley, pioneers faced their first major ascent. About a mile northwest of the Lower California Crossing of the South Platte River loomed **California Hill,** an unwelcome sight that must have appeared to the emigrants as more than just a hill. Here they would drive their livestock to pull loaded wagons up a 240-foot grade in a little over a mile and a half. At the crest was a plateau that offered a path toward the North Platte River Valley.

Major ruts were cut in California Hill by wagon trains headed to Ash Hollow and the North Platte River.

Thousands of wagons pulled by oxen straining up the hill left behind an impressive swale carved deeper during decades of erosion. Multiple swales beginning near the base appear to merge into a single impressive cut as the hill is ascended. The section of land on which California Hill is located was gifted to the Oregon-California Trails Association, which permits public access so today's visitors are able to walk in the steps of the pioneers.

California Hill is approximately 4.5 miles west of the town of Brule via US 30, the historic old Lincoln Road. A prominent marker noting the history of California Hill rests beside a turnout on the north side of the highway. A short distance beyond the marker, a rough dirt and gravel road to the north leads to an access gate for those who wish to explore the hill. A small parking space is on the west side of the road beside the gate. There were no other visitors on the four occasions we visited one of the Oregon Trail's most impressive landmarks.

11. Windlass Hill

Following the difficult climb of California Hill, pioneers traveled 18 miles along a high ridge to where they encountered the next major obstacle, a 300-foot drop so sharp some called it "perpendicular hill." The 25-degree slope would later assume

A view of Ash Hollow from atop Windlass Hill.

the name **Windlass Hill,** although there were no known entries in pioneer diaries that a windlass device was ever used to descend the hill. (A windlass is a crank-operated cylinder wrapped with a rope or chain, used to raise or lower heavy objects.)

Before attempting the descent pioneers rough-locked the back wheels of their wagons with logs so the wheels would slide rather than turn. With brakes set they used ropes to gradually lower the wagons. Additional weights such as logs were sometimes attached to drag along the ground behind a wagon and slow its descent. Negotiating a wagon down Windlass Hill required nerve and several hours of hard work. Fortunately, the oasis of Ash Hollow was only a couple of miles north and could be observed from the top of the hill.

A monument atop Windlass Hill marks the historic trail.

An interpretive shelter in the shape of a covered wagon is beside the parking lot off the entry road. A 0.75-mile paved trail leads from the parking lot to the top of Windlass Hill. The trail includes some steep sections, but benches are available for an occasional rest, and the view from the top of the hill is more than worth the effort. Markers atop the hill indicate the location of the Oregon Trail. Deciding not to hike to the top of the hill means missing what is most likely the most memorable experience of a park visit.

A heavily eroded ravine winding beside the trail marks the major path used by pioneers to descend the hill. Decades of erosion have taken such a toll on the primary downhill path of the wagons that it has become difficult to visualize how the ruts must have appeared during the era the trail was active. Indentations along the side of the hill indicate other paths taken by the emigrants. Swales made by the wagons and oxen are more easily seen during the fall.

Windlass Hill is a detached section of Ash Hollow State Historical Park. Entrance to the Windlass Hill parking area is 2.5 miles south of Ash Hollow on the west side of US 26.

12. Ash Hollow

Ash Hollow must have seemed a pleasant dream to pioneers who had by then traveled 500 miles from Independence, much of it along the treeless and featureless Platte River Valley. At Ash Hollow the emigrants were welcomed by a refuge that offered grass, flowers, trees, fruit, game for hunting, and, most important, clear spring water. The latter was especially prized because the shallow, sand-bottomed Platte River provided mostly gritty drinking water that was fine for livestock but barely palatable for humans.

The picturesque hollow is approximately 4 miles in length and bordered with white limestone cliffs averaging 250 feet in height. The base of Windlass Hill empties into the head of the hollow, whose north terminus opens a short distance from the south bank of the North Platte River. While emigrants expressed concern the hollow provided good cover for a possible American Indian attack, many decided to remain camped here for several days during which they could repair wagons, gather firewood, and enjoy some downtime before continuing on their journey.

Departing the hollow, pioneers turned west and followed the south bank of the North Platte leading to Fort Laramie. Along the way they would experience some of the Oregon Trail's most impressive landmarks in what is sometimes called "Monument Valley." Emigrant traffic to Ash Hollow waned in the latter 1850s following the discovery of gold in what is now Colorado. At that point the majority of trail traffic continued along the South Platte River as it curved south toward the newly discovered mineral riches.

Ash Hollow and nearby Windlass Hill are part of Nebraska's **Ash Hollow State Historical Park,** which offers visitors more than simply an Oregon Trail experience. The park is home to a historic 1903 stone schoolhouse (in its original location) and a visitor center with exhibits that include fossils of prehistoric creatures. The hollow was once home to camels, elephants, rhinoceroses, and horses. A cave near the visitor center was used by humans as shelter for thousands of years.

Today's visitors who depart the park head north, cross a bridge over the North Platte, and turn northwest on US 26 to follow the river along its north bank. The pioneers headed the same direction but along the river's south bank. Like the pioneers, present-day travelers will soon marvel at some of America's most impressive landscapes.

Ash Hollow State Historical Park is 3 miles south of Lewellen on US 26. From Ogallala on I-80, the park is approximately 25 miles northwest on US 26. The park is open year-round, but the visitor center is open seasonally. A Nebraska state park permit is required for park access, and a nominal fee is charged for entry to the visitor center and cave. Phone (308) 778-5651 for current information.

Trail Preservation and Education in the State Parks

City, state, and national parks play an important role in preserving historic trail remnants and landmarks while educating visitors about trail history. State parks along the Oregon Trail range from Hollenberg Pony Express Station State Historic Site in Kansas to Deschutes River State Recreation Area in Oregon. The former was once a store and tavern patronized by emigrants traveling northwest to Fort Kearny, while the latter preserves an important river crossing as pioneers neared the end of the overland portion of the trail during the early years of pioneer travel. Between these two historic locations are additional state parks devoted to telling the story of America's great western migration.

Nebraska, perhaps the state most closely associated with the Oregon Trail, is home to several of the trail's best-known landmarks including Fort Kearny, Courthouse Rock, Chimney Rock, and Scotts Bluff. Less familiar to most travelers, but considered by many pioneers as one of their most pleasant stops along the trail, is Ash Hollow. Now a Nebraska State Historical Park, Ash Hollow has been one of our favorite locations along the trail since our initial visit in 2010.

During our most recent trip to Ash Hollow, we enjoyed spending some time with park superintendent **Tamara Cooper.** Tamara was raised on Standing Rock Indian Reservation in North Dakota and later educated at the University of Nebraska at Lincoln and Nebraska Wesleyan University. Her tenure as superintendent at Ash Hollow commenced in 2017 following a stint at Buffalo Bill State Historical Park in North Platte, Nebraska.

Tamara estimates the park annually hosts 300 to 400 students, mostly 4th-graders studying state history, who arrive on school field trips. The superintendent said she has witnessed an increasing number of visits by young families, not just for the scenery, but to learn about the park in person, rather than on the internet or via a book. "That's a step in the right direction," she said. "A personal visit changes the relevancy of the history when you can experience the place where it happened." As the park's full name implies, Ash Hollow is steeped in history, and for much more than emigrant travel.

The superintendent's job is all-encompassing. Tamara gives private tours, does archiving, pays bills, engages in rangeland management, schedules meetings, cleans bathrooms, takes care of equipment repairs, and on it goes. Six months of the year she is the park's only employee.

Despite the heavy workload and relatively isolated location, Tamara enjoys the job's rewards. "In the large scope of things, it really comes down to the short amount of time you get to be the steward to the land and its place in time. It is overwhelmingly humbling to be able to say you had a part in the preservation and education of all the events and changes that have taken place here. You can only hope you did all of its history justice while you were there."

New projects are in the works at the historical park. One is a junior ranger program that focuses on the park's history and flora. Ms. Cooper is also planning the addition of signage on the park's hiking trails.

In closing, the park superintendent commented, "In the smaller scope of things, I hands down have the most beautiful office view in the state." Thanks to the country's state parks and employees like Tamara Cooper, the rest of us are able to visit these historic places and enjoy the same view, if only for a short time.

13. Rachel Pattison Grave

Estimates of deaths along the trail vary from 20,000 to 30,000, or 7 to 10 percent of emigrants who set out for the West. The dead were frequently buried wrapped in blankets below the trail, while other graves near the trail were covered with rocks and marked with wooden stakes. Most of these pioneer graves have been lost to history.

One of the trail's best-known pioneer graves is in an active cemetery at Ash Hollow. **Rachel Pattison,** an 18-year-old bride, married shortly before departing for Oregon from her Ohio home, died here on June 19, 1849. This was a year of heavy travel along the trail, much of it to the California goldfields, and cholera had become a major killer. It is assumed cholera was the likely culprit in Rachel's death.

Rachel Pattison's grave is in the front portion of the cemetery near the north entrance to Ash Hollow State Historical Park. Her weathered headstone is protected behind a glass panel near the bottom of an obelisk monument. The monument's inscription reads: "Rachel E. Pattison. Aged 18. June 19th 49." Hers is thought to be the first burial here. Other pioneers who met death at or near Ash Hollow were also buried in the cemetery, although their graves are no longer marked.

Rachel Pattison was the first pioneer to be buried at Ash Hollow Cemetery.

14. Oshkosh Country Club Swale

Heading northwest from Ash Hollow along the south bank of the North Platte River, wagon trains left depressions in the ground that remain visible today. One of these is quite unusual and of particular significance to golfers, no matter how embarrassing their handicap.

A swale of the Oregon Trail crosses the second fairway at the **Oshkosh Country Club.** This is a preview for today's travelers who will continue following the trail to Idaho and walk beside the impressive swale alongside the ninth fairway at the Oregon Trail Country Club in Soda Springs. However, it is an enjoyable experience to view the old trail near Oshkosh and appreciate that someone cared enough to leave a valuable trail remnant for others to enjoy.

Oshkosh Country Club is 3 miles south of Oshkosh on NE 27. Stop at the country club office and ask permission before setting out for a walk on the course. The swale is also visible from NE 27, which borders the west side of the course. The location is identified by a small Oregon Trail sign above a broken wagon wheel.

15. John Hollman Grave

The grave of **John Hollman** is one of the very few along the Oregon Trail that retains the original stone marker. Although difficult to read, the inscription states: "John Hollman Died June 5, 1852." Nothing else was known about this pioneer who died along the trail until the Oregon-California Trail Association decided to investigate.

John Hollman was born in 1833 in Platteville, Wisconsin. His father, Fredenck, immigrated from Germany, and his mother, Martha Thompson, was from Kentucky. The couple married in 1823 and 4 years later moved near Platteville, where all nine of their children were born.

In 1849 Fredenck, his oldest son, and a group from Platteville caught gold fever and traveled by ship to California. The two returned to Wisconsin in 1852. When friends organized a wagon train to California in order to unite with family members, John and two of his brothers joined the company. It is likely the three boys were employed as hired hands in exchange for their passage. One of the wagon train leaders, 74-year-old Alexander Hamilton Willard, had been a member of the Lewis and Clark Expedition.

According to research by the Oregon-California Trails Association, a July 28 story in the *Platteville American,* "The Fate of Many," included a letter written by 23-year-old Ellen Willard, Alexander's daughter. Addressed and dated, "Sandy Hill, Platte River, June 5, 1852," she described the death of her 19-year-old friend, John Hollman: "He was fine in the morning, got very thirsty around 11 AM. Drank from a

Original 1852 gravestone of John Hollman, who died during an 1852 journey to California.

standing pool of water and by that evening was deathly sick. He was loved by every-one on the wagon train and they were all very sad when he died."

To visit the grave, drive south from Oshkosh on NE 27, cross the North Platte River, and take the first right. The grave sits on a knoll about 0.1 mile on the right.

16. Indian Lookout Point (Frog's Head Bluff)

Emigrants on the Oregon Trail used landmarks as guideposts along the way. A land-mark for those traveling the Council Bluffs Road on the north side of the North Platte was the summit of a bluff that some travelers claimed had the appearance of a large frog with an open mouth. Several Mormon diaries noted that climbing Frog's Head Bluff offered a view of Chimney Rock, which they estimated at 20 miles distant. At this point, however, Chimney Rock was still 40 miles away, so it was more likely they were viewing Courthouse Rock and Jail Rock, about 20 miles to the south and much larger.

Being the tallest bluff in the area, it was also used by American Indians to observe the surrounding territory while searching for buffalo and other game or, perhaps, unwanted guests crossing their land. Thus the bluff was also known as **Indian Lookout Point.**

Indian Lookout Point, also known as Frog's Head Bluff, was a landmark on the north side of the North Platte River.

The bluff is 2 miles west of the town of Lisco on the north side of US 26. A pull-off with an interpretive board is a short distance east of the landmark.

17. Ancient Bluff Ruins

Ancient Bluff Ruins, three buttes clustered along the north side of the North Platte River, caught the attention of emigrants following the Council Bluffs Road that paralleled the river's north bank. The formation was also noted by pioneers following the south bank, although to a lesser extent. Near Ancient Bluff Ruins travelers following the north bank often caught their first glimpse of distant Courthouse Rock.

Brigham Young and his party of 144 men, three wives, and two small boys camped near here on May 22 and 23 during their 1847 journey to Utah. Exploring the formation, Young and some companions reportedly climbed the highest bluff and wrote their names on a buffalo skull.

Ancient Bluff Ruins was reportedly climbed by Brigham Young, whose party camped near here.

The trail landmark's unusual name apparently originated with European converts being reminded of castles, towers, and ruins in their homeland. Ancient Bluff Ruins is just north of US 26, approximately 5 miles southeast of the town of Broadwater.

18. Amanda Lamme (Lamin) Grave

Nebraska settlers in the latter 1800s discovered a headstone that was in pieces after being trampled by cattle. Assembling the pieces they came up with the following inscription: "Amanda Consort of M.J. Lamin of Devonshire, Eng. Born Feb. 22, 1822 Died June 23, 1850, of Cholera."

The broken marker was replaced in 1912 with a two-sided granite monument inscribed on the west-facing side with "Oregon Trail marked by State of Nebraska 1912/Trail passed 285 feet north of this point." The inscription from the previous stone was placed on the opposite side.

Research by the Nebraska State Historical Society determined the correct spelling of Amanda's last name as Lamme, and that she was born in Missouri rather than England. Other information on the stone marker appeared correct. One theory of the mix-up is that the settlers who discovered the original stone did their best but unknowingly assembled pieces of two broken headstones.

The grave's remains belonged to Amanda Maupin, who was born on February 22, 1822, in Boone County, Missouri. Amanda, along with her husband, daughters, and relatives, departed Missouri in April 1850 for California. Cholera caught up with Amanda, and she died on June 23 after falling ill the prior day. She was buried in a grove of trees with a temporary wooden marker.

A June 30, 1850, entry in the journal of pioneer Micha Littleton noted his observation of a grave marked "Amanda Lamme, June 23, age 28, Boon Co., MO." It is assumed this was a temporary wooden marker her husband had initially placed on Amanda's grave. In a near repeat of the Susan Haile story, Amanda's husband, Jack, returned east to purchase a more permanent marker. One version has him returning with another wagon train. Another says he returned using a wheelbarrow to haul a granite marker. After replacing the wooden marker with the marble headstone, husband Jack later in the fall caught up with his family in California.

Amanda Lamme's Grave is on private property and not open to the public. A Nebraska historical marker beside the road is in the general area of the grave. The marker is on US 385/NE 92 just past the junction of these two roads southeast of Bridgeport.

19. Courthouse Rock and Jail Rock

Nebraska's Panhandle, home to the great monoliths that emigrants found fascinating, was once a huge plain hundreds of feet higher in elevation than today. The land here built up over millions of years as it accumulated multiple deposits of sand and mud flowing east from the uplifted Rocky Mountains. This was supplemented with windblown ash from volcanic activity to the west. Most of the soft, porous land gradually eroded away leaving scattered islands protected by resistant limestone caps. Remnants of this process comprise the natural wonders that greeted pioneers in the 1800s, and travelers today as they follow the North Platte River from Ash Hollow to the Wyoming border.

Courthouse Rock, a huge sandstone butte pioneers often referred to as the "Courthouse" or "Castle," was the first of the great monuments they encountered. Topping out at 400 feet above the Platte River Valley, the Courthouse could be seen during several days of travel prior to the trail passing about 5 miles north of the promontory. Named for an appearance many pioneers considered similar to that of the courthouse in St. Louis or, perhaps, courthouses back home, the Courthouse was paired with **Jail Rock**, a smaller neighbor a short distance to the east. While Courthouse Rock found its way into many pioneer journals, its smaller neighbor was seldom mentioned.

The large dimensions of Courthouse Rock combined with the scarcity of nearby landmarks with which it could be compared caused pioneers to underestimate their distance from the monument. As a result, those who were sufficiently entranced and decided to walk to the butte for a closer examination discovered the trek required considerably more time and effort than anticipated.

Courthouse Rock (left) and Jail Rock were major landmarks on the historic trail.

Courthouse Rock and Jail Rock are 5 miles south of Bridgeport on NE 88. An access road leads to a parking area and a walking trail to the base of the monument. No facilities are available at the site.

20. Chimney Rock

Chimney Rock, the best known of the monuments in the Nebraska Panhandle, is to the Oregon Trail what the Golden Gate Bridge is to San Francisco and the Eiffel Tower is to Paris. Mention the first and most individuals immediately link it to the second. The "Chimney," as many pioneers referred to it, isn't as massive as Courthouse Rock and not nearly as important to pioneer travel as South Pass, but the unusual monolith, shaped in the form of an overturned funnel, was noted in more pioneer journals than any other landmark along the trail. Today it remains the iconic symbol of the pioneers' trek west and was chosen by the Nebraska governor to adorn the state's quarter.

Pioneers heading west along the trail got their first view of Chimney Rock when they were still 30 to 40 miles away. At the time the monument's spire was 30 to 50 feet taller than today. As with Courthouse Rock, the distance to Chimney Rock could be deceiving, and emigrants were often surprised how long it took to arrive near the landmark, where they would often camp.

The Pony Express Rides Again

The **Pony Express** remains an iconic part of the nation's history despite lasting only 18 months (April 1860–October 1861) and losing a pile of money for its owners. Covering nearly 2,000 miles in 10 days between St. Joseph, Missouri, and Sacramento, California, Pony Express riders traced a large portion of the route used by pioneers headed west. The firm utilized nearly 150 stations and employed eighty riders who were each expected to cover 75 to 100 miles per day.

Although completion of the transcontinental telegraph in October 1861 put the company out of business, the spirit of the Pony Express continues in the form of an annual Pony Express Commemorative Re-Ride during the first two weeks of June. Over 750 riders participate in riding the same historic route day and night for ten days. While original riders like Buffalo Bill Cody and Pony Bob Haslam rode up to 100 miles per day, today's individual riders cover less ground as they must contend with vehicle traffic. The riders also often spend time at stops to talk with spectators. That proved the case with the two of us during a visit to Scotts Bluff National Monument.

Scotts Bluff is one of the riders' many stops, and we were fortunate to be at the monument's visitor center during a beautiful June day when rider Max Cewiezel stopped to change horses. During his stopover Max took a few moments to talk with monument visitors about the Pony Express and the National Pony Express Association's re-ride. He also exhibited the leather mochila filled with letters the riders were carrying for delivery to Sacramento.

Each year the National Pony Express Association posts a schedule of the upcoming ride on its website, www.nationalponyexpress.org.

Rider Max Cewiezel heads out of Scotts Bluff for his next stop on the Pony Express Re-Ride.

Chimney Rock was the most noted landmark on the Oregon Trail.

The Chimney Rock Visitor Center, with exhibits and media presentations, is near the town of Bayard, 1.5 miles south of NE 92 on Chimney Rock Road. The visitor center patio offers an excellent view of Chimney Rock. While visitors are permitted to walk to the base of the monument, the center advises against it for safety reasons. (Also keep in mind some residents consider the rattlesnake the state reptile.) An interesting cemetery with the graves of early settlers is near the visitor center. An admission fee is charged for entry to the visitor center. Call (308) 586-2581 for information.

21. Rebecca Winters Grave

Rebecca Winters was a 50-year-old woman who, along with her husband, Hiram, was on the way to Utah in 1852 when she contracted cholera and died near Scotts Bluff on August 15. Rebecca was buried by her husband and a friend in a particularly deep grave beside the trail. The body was wrapped in blankets and wooden planks were placed at the bottom of the grave and atop the deceased. The grave was then decorated with a partial wagon wheel rim bent to appear as a monument stone. On one side of the rim, Winters's friend inscribed "Rebecca Winters, Age 50."

Fifty years passed without much notice of the grave until, in the early 1900s, the Burlington Northern Railroad laid tracks nearby. After requesting permission from

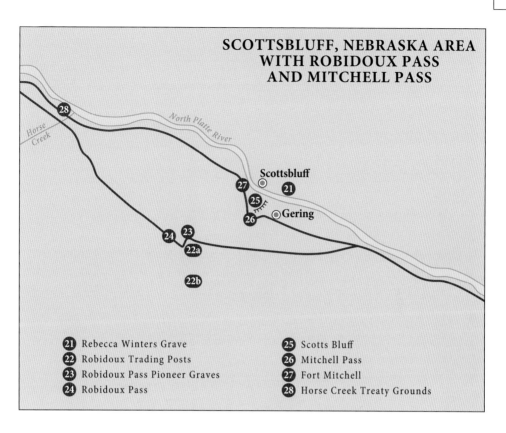

SCOTTSBLUFF, NEBRASKA AREA
WITH ROBIDOUX PASS
AND MITCHELL PASS

21 Rebecca Winters Grave	**25** Scotts Bluff
22 Robidoux Trading Posts	**26** Mitchell Pass
23 Robidoux Pass Pioneer Graves	**27** Fort Mitchell
24 Robidoux Pass	**28** Horse Creek Treaty Grounds

family members, in 1995 the Burlington Northern had archaeologists move the grave a short distance away from the tracks in an effort to increase visitor safety. Ms. Winters's remains were transferred to a mahogany casket for the reburial.

The Rebecca Winters grave is 2 miles east of the town of Scottsbluff via US 26. Turn south at South Beltline Highway East. The grave is on the left, just prior to crossing the railroad tracks.

22. Robidoux Trading Posts

By 1849 the main trail across **Robidoux Pass** had been graced with a trading post consisting of a log cabin and nearby tepees. The cabin included a store where emigrants could purchase or trade for supplies, including bad whiskey. It also housed the only blacksmith shop between Fort Kearny and Fort Laramie, allowing pioneers to have their livestock shod and wagons repaired. According to emigrant journals, the entirety of the business was in a one-room building, half of which was devoted to the blacksmith operation. The facility had been expanded somewhat by the following season.

The trading post was operated by one or more members of the Robidoux clan, the patriarch of whom was instrumental in the founding of St. Joseph, Missouri. The family consisted of a collection of enterprising individuals eager to make a buck. Its members popped up on occasion from Missouri to the southern Rocky Mountains.

In late 1850 or early 1851, proprietors of the trading post constructed a new facility at the mouth of a canyon about a mile off the main trail. The first post continued in operation during at least a portion of the 1851 season but had been abandoned by the time travelers passed through in 1852. Travel along the road declined considerably in 1851 when construction on Mitchell Pass allowed wagon access on a trail nearer the river. In any event, the primary interest of the Robidoux family remained trading with the American Indians for buffalo robes and beaver pelts to be shipped back East. Business with the emigrants was viewed as a bonus.

The former Robidoux trading post locations are approximately 8 miles southwest of Gering and accessible by personal vehicle via gravel roads. The early trading post

The replica of Robidoux's second trading post has been moved from its original location.

site is marked with a wooden sign, monuments, and a fence. Nothing remains at the second trading post site, which is on private land. A reconstructed second Robidoux trading post is on land owned by the city of Gering. To view the reconstructed post, drive south on Five Rocks Road for 0.5 mile from the intersection of M Street and Five Rocks Road. At D Street, make a right. Follow this gravel county road approximately 0.8 mile. The reconstructed trading post is in a field on the right side of the road. Gering's Five Rocks Amphitheater is on the left side of the road.

To access the first trading post site, head south from Gering on Five Rocks Road and turn west on Robidoux Road. The site is approximately 8 miles west on the often dusty gravel road, marked by a wooden sign on a bluff to the left.

23. Robidoux Pass Pioneer Graves

On the north side of Robidoux Road, between the site of the fur trader's first trading post and Robidoux Pass, is a fenced area with four metal crosses and a stone monument. The four crosses represent unknown pioneers who died near the site. A brass plaque attached to the stone monument reads: "Honoring These And All The Thousands Who Lie In Nameless Graves Along The Trail. Faith And Courage Such As Theirs Made America. May Ours Preserve It."

A historical marker placed at the site by the Oregon-California Trails Association tells the story of **Fleming Dunn,** a 49er headed for the California goldfields who died nearby. The original grave marker placed by members of his wagon train lasted into the 1920s but subsequently disappeared. Dunn was traveling with his brother, Ellis, and a group of Illinois men who called themselves "The Peoria Pioneers." He was married with two daughters, one of whom died at the age of 1. On June 13, 1849, Dunn died of cholera at the age of 26. An already sad story only gets worse as Dunn's 18-month-old daughter died of cholera about 2 months after her father's death, while a month later his widow died of dysentery.

24. Robidoux Pass

During the 1840s emigrant wagon trains following the Oregon Trail in present-day western Nebraska were blocked from continuing along the south bank of the North Platte by the massive bluffs and adjoining badlands that reached the river. While a gap near the river at Scotts Bluff had long been used by trappers and missionaries, attempting to squeeze wagons through the narrow passage was another matter.

To bypass the lengthy obstruction, emigrants detoured toward the southwest through the scenic Gering Valley, which offered water for drinking, grass for livestock, and wood for cooking. Then it was up a grade to cross 4,554-foot **Robidoux Pass.**

Robidoux Pass shown here was used by pioneers until Mitchell Pass opened for wagons in 1851.

From this point the pioneers gained a panoramic view of what lay ahead in addition to where they had traveled during the previous several days.

The trail over Robidoux Pass remained the primary route of Oregon-bound emigrants until 1851 when Mitchell Pass, between Scotts Bluff and South Bluff, was widened and leveled to allow access for wagon traffic. Even then, Robidoux Pass remained in use, just not as heavily as during the 1840s.

Robidoux Pass is a little over a mile west of Robidoux's first trading post and the pioneer graves. As the gravel road takes a sharp turn to the south at the top of the hill, exit on the two-track. Park and walk to the fenced monument directly ahead.

25. Scotts Bluff

Pioneers were awed by the immense bulk and majesty of Courthouse Rock, but the best was down the road. Thirty-five miles ahead, beyond Chimney Rock and other assorted scenic wonders, was another remnant of the high plains so massive it forced a major detour for wagon trains following the south bank of the North Platte River. This huge sandstone remnant was **Scotts Bluff,** named for **Hiram Scott,** an unlucky employee of the Rocky Mountain Fur Company who grew ill and died near the bluff in 1828 after being deserted by his travel companions. Or perhaps he died from a wound suffered in a conflict with the Blackfeet. Some say he died at a different location and crawled to the bluff where his remains were found. Regardless, by dying near this previously unnamed bluff, Hiram ensured his name would assume a permanent place in Oregon Trail history.

At twice the height of Courthouse Rock, Scotts Bluff was and remains an impressive piece of nature's work. It rises 800 feet above the valley floor with a composition similar to Courthouse Rock and Chimney Rock. While current reference to Scotts Bluff applies to the large bluff on the north side of the highway, during pioneer times the term generally referred to the entire remnant from the badlands adjoining the river to 10 miles south where the extension terminates.

History buffs and today's travelers are fortunate that Scotts Bluff was established as a national monument in 1919. The monument visitor center is home to a small museum that includes an impressive collection of sketches, paintings, and photographs by famed artist William Henry Jackson, who first passed through here in 1866. While the National Park Service owns the originals, they are considered fragile and reproductions are on display in the visitor center.

Scotts Bluff National Monument offers living history programs during the summer months.

Volunteers Keep the Wheels Rolling

Volunteers are vital to the functioning of most interpretive centers and museums, many of which operate on a shoestring budget with a skeleton staff of paid employees. Without volunteers these institutions would need to reduce the hours they are open to the public and, in many instances, offer fewer exhibits and interpretive programs.

During a lengthy stop at **Scotts Bluff National Monument** in western Nebraska, we had the opportunity to talk with two individuals involved with the monument's volunteer program. National Park Service ranger **Ittai (Ty) Levine,** the monument's volunteer coordinator, told us the park has six regular volunteers plus several other individuals on call as substitutes or for special events. Ty said he looks for people who demonstrate a dedication to the park and an interest in the environment. At Scotts Bluff volunteers help staff the information desk, participate in living history programs, inspect the trails, and assist at the entrance gate. A few individuals even offer to help with maintenance. Most volunteers are retired, but college students and working individuals sometimes volunteer on weekends and holidays when the park is at its busiest.

National Park Service volunteer Doug Kent enjoys another day helping visitors at Scotts Bluff National Monument.

Douglas Kent is one of Scotts Bluff National Monument's regular volunteers. Doug, who was 81 years old at the time of our meeting, was born and raised in Scottsbluff and began volunteering at the park 3 years after selling his wholesale magazine distribution business in 2011. For most of his years as a volunteer, Doug drove the park shuttle on the narrow, winding road that connects the visitor center with the summit of Scotts Bluff. More recently he had been working behind the information desk, staffing the entrance gate, and offering assistance to visitors at various locations in the monument.

It was obvious during our conversation that Doug enjoys interacting with park visitors. He related that his greatest satisfaction comes from working with people. He talks to visitors about the park's history and geology, along with other places they may want to see during their trip. He said he particularly enjoys the people he works with in the park, who include him as part of their team. He typically walks from 10,000 to 20,000 steps during the day, making the volunteer hours serve as a way to maintain his physical and mental fitness. As we parted Doug commented, "My experience as a volunteer has been phenomenal." The parks and their visitors owe a debt of gratitude to dedicated volunteers like Doug Kent.

The top of Scotts Bluff is accessible via a paved road or hiking trail.

The bluff summit, accessible via either a unique 1.6-mile auto road or a walking path, offers outstanding views of Chimney Rock, Mitchell Pass, and the valley floor. A 0.5-mile trail at the summit provides access to the North Overlook with its views of the North Platte River Valley, including the badlands that blocked wagon travel along the river's south bank. A popular walking trail from the visitor center leads past replica wagons to impressive Oregon Trail swales cut by thousands of pioneer wagons rolling through Mitchell Pass on their way to Fort Laramie.

Scotts Bluff is a short distance west of Gering via M Street and Old Oregon Trail. Consider spending an extra day in the area to allow sufficient time for exploring the monument and nearby Robidoux Pass and Wildcat Hills.

26. Mitchell Pass

The narrow, winding gap between Scotts Bluff and South Bluff proved unsuitable for wagon travel prior to its widening and leveling in 1850. It is unclear who undertook the work, but is generally believed to have been either US Army personnel from Fort Laramie or employees of the American Fur Company, the latter hoping to benefit by luring business away from the competing operation on the trail over Robidoux

Mitchell Pass allowed wagon trains to remain near the North Platte River at Scotts Bluff.

Pass. Within a year of the improvements, a majority of Oregon Trail wagon trains had altered their route and were traveling over **Mitchell Pass,** which was nearer the river. The pass was not called by its current name until Fort Mitchell was constructed nearby in 1864.

Wagons using Mitchell Pass did not follow the current auto road, but rather paralleled the road until passing a short distance in front of and beyond today's Scotts Bluff National Monument visitor center. The trail then made a bend to the north to pass through the gap before turning northwest. Today's visitors can stroll a paved walk from the visitor center to reach the path of the Oregon Trail as it squeezed though Mitchell Pass.

27. Fort Mitchell

A number of army posts were constructed throughout the frontier during the period of westward expansion. While Fort Kearny and Fort Laramie became major posts that operated for lengthy periods, the majority were small and in service for only a short time. **Fort Mitchell,** located just west of Scotts Bluff, constructed in 1864 and abandoned around 1867, fell into the latter group.

Major American Indian skirmishes engulfed the plains in the early 1860s in retaliation for numerous atrocities against Indigenous people. The battles intensified following the Sand Creek Massacre, during which soldiers killed 150 unarmed men, women, and children in an American Indian village in present-day Colorado.

Fort Mitchell, briefly called Camp Shuman, was constructed on the North Platte River as an outpost of Fort Laramie to help protect the area from American Indian attacks. The Civil War had drawn regular soldiers from the western forts, resulting in Fort Mitchell being built and manned by one company of the 11th Ohio Volunteer Cavalry. The fort was unusual in that its buildings were constructed of sod with their back walls forming a 180-by-100-foot rectangular barricade. Not a lot is known about the fort, but sketches by William Henry Jackson display the sod stockade walls, one sentinel tower, and an adjoining log stockade for the horses.

The soldiers of Fort Mitchell joined soldiers from other forts in a few major American Indian battles, but their daily duties primarily consisted of patrolling the area and escorting the many wagon trains, freight wagons, and stagecoaches to the next fort. When the Civil War ended in 1865, regular soldiers returned to posts in the West, and the Ohio volunteers were replaced by a company of the 18th Infantry.

There is no known record of Fort Mitchell after February 1867, and the date of its abandonment is uncertain. One theory is the fort was no longer needed once regular soldiers returned to the western forts following the Civil War. Another is that the fort was abandoned following the Fort Laramie Treaty of 1868. Whichever is true, Fort Mitchell did not survive for long, and its sod structures soon disintegrated into the face of the earth.

Fort Mitchell's former location was determined during a 1909 area survey. The site is now on private land, but a roadside interpretive display indicates the location and describes the fort's history. Additional displays focus on the Oregon Trail and Pony Express. A pull-off for the interpretive displays is on the south side of NE 92 between the west end of the North Platte River bridge and Old Oregon Trail out of Scotts Bluff National Monument.

28. Horse Creek Treaty Grounds

An 1851 treaty council arranged by the US government was designed to quell the conflict among tribes of the Northern Plains and allow for safe passage of emigrants through American Indian lands. Originally scheduled to take place at Fort Laramie, the meeting was moved to **Horse Creek** due to the large number of American Indians who decided to attend. The treaty is officially known as the Fort Laramie Treaty of 1851.

Fort Laramie Treaty of 1851

Wagon trains started rolling through the plains in the early 1840s, with emigrants killing bison and other wild game that had long been American Indians' primary food source. In the early years of the trail when traffic was fairly light, the loss of game was limited and not a major concern, resulting in generally cordial relations between the pioneers and American Indians. As the number of travelers picked up in the late 1840s, the killing of game became a sore spot leading to skirmishes with American Indians who considered the emigrants as interlopers. Individuals who lived with both groups—fur traders, missionaries, Indian agents—worked to organize a meeting with the tribes to negotiate safe passage for emigrants through Indigenous land.

The US Congress authorized a treaty council with the Plains American Indians in 1851, with **Fort Laramie** selected as the location and tribes invited to arrive by September 1. Fort Laramie was unable to accommodate the more than 10,000 American Indians who accepted the offer. The treaty site was relocated about 30 miles east, to the mouth of Horse Creek on the North Platte River, resulting in the eventual agreement often being referred to as the "**Horse Creek Treaty.**" The Mandan, Crow, Brule Sioux, Arikara, Rees, Cheyenne, Gros Ventre, Hidatsa, and Snake were present. Oglala Sioux, Assiniboine, Arapaho, and Shoshone also arrived although they had not been invited. The Apache, Comanche, and Kiowa were invited but refused to attend. American Indian camps on the treaty grounds were dispersed to limit contact as some tribes had been at war for generations.

Representatives of the US government included fur trapper Thomas Fitzpatrick, who at the time was Indian agent to the Sioux; David D. Mitchell, superintendent of Indian Affairs at St. Louis; Jesuit Father Pierre-Jean De Smet, who for years had been involved with the American Indians; mountain man Jim Bridger; and explorer John C. Fremont. One thousand soldiers had been requested to help maintain the peace, but only about 300 were sent.

The final treaty specified the rights and responsibilities of both the American Indians and the US government. The agreement stipulated tribes would abstain from hostilities against one another; the US government had the right to establish roads and posts on Indian Territory; the US government would protect tribal resources and hunting grounds, and provide tracts of land or territories where each Indian nation would reside; and the US government would pay the Indian nations $50,000 in goods annually for 10 years for the right to cross their land.

On September 17, 1851, David D. Mitchell and Thomas Fitzpatrick signed the treaty for the United States, and twenty-one chiefs signed or affixed their marks for the Plains nations. The US Senate ratified the treaty on May 24, 1852, but the agreement was never published as ratified in the US Statutes at Large, resulting in some question as to its validity.

The US government almost immediately broke the treaty by failing to protect tribal hunting grounds. In addition, only a single monetary payment was made to the Indian nations. Tribes remained reasonably peaceful until 1858 when gold was discovered in Colorado, resulting in a mad rush of gold seekers and others who coveted the "protected" land. The eventual result was the American Indian War that broke out in 1864.

A roadside exhibit tells the story of the Fort Laramie Treaty of 1851, also known as the Horse Creek Treaty. The treaty grounds are on private property.

A roadside interpretive exhibit with plaques describes the gathering and the treaty's meaning for the American Indian nations and emigrants. One marker is a map illustrating the locations of various groups and individuals scattered among the treaty grounds. The exhibit is on the north side of US 26 about 4 miles west of the town of Morrill. The actual treaty site is at the mouth of Horse Creek where it empties into the North Platte River, on private property 2.75 miles in front of the exhibit site.

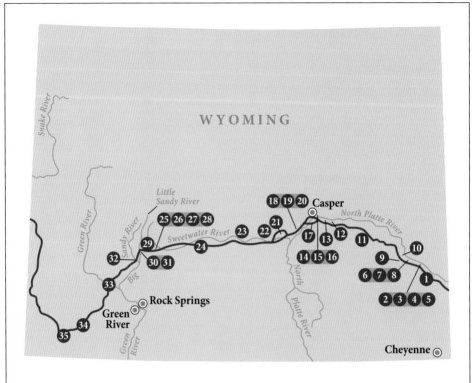

WYOMING

1. Grattan Massacre Site
2. Fort Platte
3. Fort Laramie
4. Mary Homsley Grave
5. Bedlam Ruts
6. Register Cliff
7. Guernsey Ruts
8. Lucindy Rollins Grave
9. Warm Springs
10. Cold Spring and Rifle Pit Hill
11. Ayres Natural Bridge
12. Ada Magill Grave
13. Reshaw's Bridge
14. Mormon Ferry
15. Guinard Bridge
16. Fort Caspar
17. Bessemer Bend
18. Rock Avenue
19. Willow Spring
20. Prospect Hill
21. Independence Rock
22. Devil's Gate
23. Split Rock
24. Ice Slough
25. South Pass
26. Oregon Buttes
27. Pacific Springs
28. South Pass Overlook
29. False Parting of the Ways
30. Parting of the Ways
31. Little Sandy Crossing
32. Big Sandy Crossing
33. Lombard Ferry
34. Church Butte
35. Fort Bridger

WYOMING

After negotiating their way around or through Scotts Bluff (following the 1851 opening of Mitchell Pass), pioneers entered today's southeastern Wyoming and headed to Fort Laramie, initially a fur trading post that was converted into a military post after being acquired by the federal government in 1849. Here emigrants could rest, acquire provisions, and take advantage of blacksmith facilities that were few and far between in the early days of the trail.

Although emigrants suffered accidents and health issues during travel along the Platte River Valley, the trail was mostly level with water to drink and grass to feed livestock. Ahead were more serious challenges including multiple river crossings, alkaline water that sickened humans and killed livestock, wide temperature variations, and rocky ground that proved brutal for hooves, human feet, and wagon wheels. On a positive note, the great killer, cholera, had abated somewhat by the time the emigrants reached this stage of their trip.

William Henry Jackson, *Platte Bridge* COURTESY OF FORT CASPAR MUSEUM

Departing Fort Laramie the emigrants headed northwest following the North Platte, with many stopping along the way to etch their name, home state, and date in sandstone near a campground at Register Cliff and, a little farther on, to bathe and wash clothes at Warm Springs. The main trail remained on the south side of the North Platte River, requiring wagon trains to cross to the north bank near present-day Casper where the river took a turn to the southwest. The crossing was a difficult ford that provided opportunities for entrepreneurs to make a buck by operating ferries and constructing bridges. Leaving behind the river they had been following for hundreds of miles, travelers hit a dry and dusty patch to reach the Sweetwater River. The winding Sweetwater required numerous crossings along which the pioneers encountered a string of the Oregon Trail's most storied landmarks including Independence Rock, Devil's Gate, Split Rock, and the unusual Ice Slough. A little farther was South Pass, the wide and gentle saddle over which pioneer wagons crossed the Continental Divide.

About 20 miles after crossing South Pass, emigrants arrived at "Parting of the Ways," where it became decision time. Wagon trains headed to the Salt Lake Valley and California, along with some emigrants whose destination was Oregon, continued southwest along the main trail to Fort Bridger. Other Oregon-bound pioneers chose to save about 45 miles and a couple of days' travel by following the Sublette Cutoff (also called the "Greenwood Cutoff") that led almost due west. The cutoff opened in 1844 with 50 miles of waterless desert travel that led to the Bear Lake Valley and rejoined the main trail.

Those continuing to Fort Bridger discovered what many considered a fairly depressing trading post, although they were able to purchase limited supplies, trade exhausted livestock, and undertake repair work on their wagons. The fort, located at a junction of multiple trails, experienced an interesting life (and demise). Mormons and many California-bound wagon trains continued south from Fort Bridger toward the Great Salt Lake. Pioneers seeking a new home in Oregon who had chosen to avoid the desert travel of the Sublette Cutoff headed northwest toward the Bear Lake Valley in present-day Idaho.

1. Grattan Massacre Site

In August 1854 a young and inexperienced West Point graduate initiated an armed conflict that resulted in two decades of war with the Sioux nations. The one-sided battle that became known as the **Grattan Massacre** resulted in the deaths of **Second Lieutenant John Grattan** and all twenty-nine enlisted men under his command.

The problem began with a sick cow that lagged behind a Mormon wagon train headed to Utah. The cow ended up in a nearby Brule Sioux camp, where it became the main course for dinner for American Indians waiting for promised government goods that were long overdue.

A complaint by the Mormons resulted in Grattan and a detachment of over two dozen enlisted volunteers riding from Fort Laramie to the American Indian village and demanding the surrender of the guilty party, who would be taken back to Fort Laramie. The trouble commenced after the demand was refused. Although it is uncertain which side fired the first shot, the soldiers were vastly outnumbered and the conflict was soon over.

Unfortunately, Standing Bear, the village head, who had experienced good relations with the military, was shot during the conflict and died within several days. This enraged the American Indians, who subsequently raided the area around Fort Laramie.

While relations with the American Indians had deteriorated from the first years of travel along the Oregon Trail, the 1854 action involving Grattan's unfortunate visit to the Brule Sioux village lit a powder keg that set off two decades of conflict.

A granite monument noting the conflict is 0.5 mile from the Grattan Massacre battle site, which is on private property. Driving west on US 26/85, turn south in Lingle on WY 154 and then right just south of town on WY 157. The monument is on the right (north) about a mile after crossing the North Platte River.

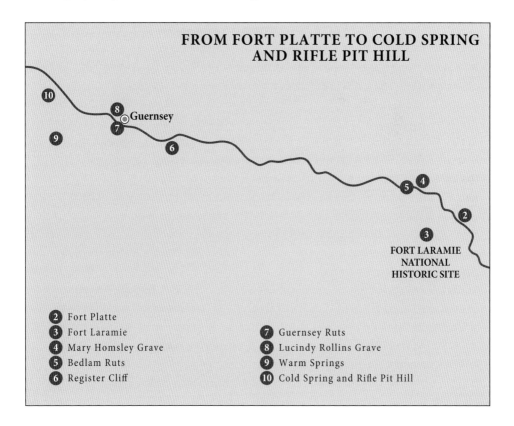

FROM FORT PLATTE TO COLD SPRING AND RIFLE PIT HILL

2 Fort Platte
3 Fort Laramie
4 Mary Homsley Grave
5 Bedlam Ruts
6 Register Cliff

7 Guernsey Ruts
8 Lucindy Rollins Grave
9 Warm Springs
10 Cold Spring and Rifle Pit Hill

2. Fort Platte

Fort William, built in 1834 as a predecessor to Fort Laramie, faced competition in 1840 when fur trader Lancaster Lupton constructed **Fort Platte** on the south bank of the North Platte River less than a mile from Fort William. Lupton was a West Point graduate and former lieutenant in the US Army, who in the mid-1830s had built a trading post between today's Laramie, Wyoming, and Santa Fe, New Mexico.

While Fort William had been constructed of vertical cottonwood logs, Lupton's Fort Platte was a more substantial adobe structure with walls 4 feet thick and 20 feet high. Approximately a dozen buildings plus a corral with a capacity of up to 200 animals were within the walls.

By the time Lupton completed Fort Platte, a deteriorating Fort William was in the hands of its third owner, the American Fur Company. With deep pockets, the firm decided to meet its new competition by constructing an adobe trading post it named Fort John.

By 1843 Fort Platte had been sold to Bernard Pratte and Jean Pierre Cabanne, who continued its operation until 1845 when they abandoned the fort and moved the business 8 miles southeast to Fort Bernard. Aubrey Haines, author and Yellowstone National Park historian, commented that Fort Platte "was probably never more than a small, shabby post of traders whose principal stock was whiskey."

Nothing remains of Fort Platte other than a monument at or near the site of the former fort. The monument is on the north side of WY 160, about 2 miles northeast of the entrance road to Fort Laramie National Historic Site.

3. Fort Laramie

From its birth as a small trading post near the confluence of the Laramie and North Platte Rivers, **Fort Laramie** would grow to become one of the most storied military posts of the nineteenth century. The initial post, Fort William, consisted of small wooden buildings surrounded by a 15-foot-high stockade constructed in 1834 from cottonwood trees. During its relatively short life serving as a trading post for buffalo robes, the fort welcomed luminaries such as **Kit Carson, Marcus Whitman, Jim Bridger,** and **Father De Smet.**

Fort William quickly cycled through a new group of owners before being purchased in 1836 by the American Fur Company. The near monopoly ended in 1840 when a fur trader from Colorado built a competing post near what had become an aging Fort William. This, in turn, forced the American Fur Company to ditch the old fort and construct a more substantial adobe post it named Fort John. By 1845 the trade in buffalo robes was past its peak and the competing trading post, Fort Platte,

The bachelor officer quarters at Fort Laramie was built in 1849 and is the oldest standing military building in Wyoming.

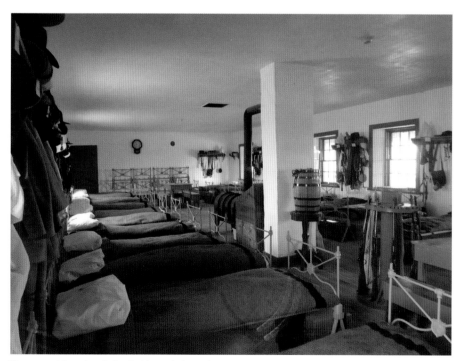

The second-floor dorm in the Fort Laramie barracks.

was abandoned. Fort John then became a mostly seasonal business catering to pioneers passing through on their way to Oregon, California, and the Salt Lake Valley.

Wanting to offer protection for the increasing flow of emigrants heading west, the government began building a series of military posts along the trail. In 1849 Fort John was purchased by the US Army and converted from a trading post to a military post, a new mission that would last until the fort was abandoned in 1890. The purchase also resulted in renaming the post "Fort Laramie," although both Fort William and Fort John had often been referred to by that name.

Following the fort purchase, US Army personnel began constructing new buildings including quarters for officers and soldiers, a guardhouse, stables, and a bakery. Unlike the trading posts that preceded it, Fort Laramie as a military post had what might be called an open floor plan that consisted of a group of buildings not enclosed by a stockade. Old Fort John fell into disrepair and had disappeared by the early 1860s.

Fort Laramie became a national monument in 1938, with the designation changed to national historic site in 1960. With Fort William, Fort Platte, and Fort John long gone, the National Park Service primarily interprets the site as it was during its military days rather than the earlier fur trading period. Today's fort includes both ruins, or foundations, along with restored structures including the captain's quarters, commissary storehouse, old bakery, bachelor officer quarters, cavalry barracks, and more.

Fort Laramie and the earlier trading posts served as important stops for emigrants on the Oregon, California, and Mormon Trails. After its purchase by the federal government, the fort became a force for stabilizing this region of the country. It remains one of the best stops for today's travelers wanting to experience the historic trails. Allow at least a half day to explore the fort, admire the military bridge, walk the Bedlam Ruts, and view the grave of Mary Homsley. Better yet, take a lunch and spend the day.

Fort Laramie National Historic Site is in southeastern Wyoming. Take US 26 into the small town of Fort Laramie, then turn west onto WY 160 and drive 3 miles to the national historic site.

4. Mary Homsley Grave

Mary Homsley was headed to Oregon with her husband and three children when an epidemic of measles spread among most of the children and a few of the adults. Mary and her young son became infected, and both suffered for several days with a fever. As they crossed a river near Fort Laramie (either the Laramie or the North Platte), the Homsley wagon overturned and Mary and the baby fell into the cold water. Both were rescued, but Mary's condition worsened and she soon died. Her husband carved the following inscription into a piece of sandstone: "Mary E.

Homsley, died June 10, 1852, age 28."
The baby died several weeks later.

Mary Elizabeth Oden was born in 1824 and in 1841 married Benjamin Homsley in Warren County, Missouri. Benjamin was a farmer and blacksmith 11 years older than Mary. In April 1852 the Homsley family, along with Mary's parents, ten brothers and sisters, and their family members, packed up and headed to Oregon.

It must have been a depressing trip for the families. Shortly after Mary died,

Mary Homsley's original gravestone, protected within the current monument.

two other family members died of cholera, and then they lost their baby boy. Benjamin Homsley made it to Oregon, raised his two daughters, and died at the age of 92.

Exiting Fort Laramie National Historic Site, turn right on the paved road and drive 1 mile to just beyond the cemetery on the right. Take the first sharp left and follow the left fork for 1.6 miles. Turn right on the first gravel road and drive 0.2 mile to where a sign points to the gravesite. While a drivable two-track road leads to the gravesite, it is preferable to park and walk the 250 steps to the grave.

5. Bedlam Ruts

Excellent swales remain from thousands of pioneer wagons pulling northwest out of Fort Laramie toward Register Cliff. The trail depressions here were named for "Old Bedlam," the bachelor officer quarters in Fort Laramie, which could be viewed from the hill on which the swales are located. The historic trail is identified by posts that can be seen in both directions from an information panel enclosed by a wooden railing.

The Bedlam Ruts outside Fort Laramie can be seen heading up the hill to the right of the interpretive sign.

For access to the ruts, use the directions noted in the Mary Homsley Grave entry. The two sites are near each other and accessed using the same road. Rather than turn right on the first gravel road that leads to the Homsley grave, continue straight another 0.4 mile to the Bedlam Ruts parking lot.

Danger Along the Trail

By some estimates from 7 to 10 percent of pioneers died during travel along the Oregon Trail. While large wagon trains sometimes included a doctor who could set broken bones and remove bullets, medicines were limited and those that were available, including castor oil, peppermint oil, camphor, citric acid, whiskey, and morphine, were often ineffective in solving the underlying problem. Wagon trains without a doctor were considerably worse off but could seek help from the doctor at a military post, if one was near.

Considering the dangers, it is remarkable how many emigrants successfully made their way to Oregon. The pioneers lived with mosquitoes, flies, body lice, and ticks. Diets were unbalanced, lacking in fruits and vegetables. Clothing was often unsuitable for the conditions, and people were frequently sleeping on the cold, wet ground. Heavy dust irritated the eyes, nose, throat, and lungs.

Accidents and carelessness often had terrible consequences. Children and adults were run over by wagon wheels. People and draft animals drowned during difficult river crossings. Most emigrants were farmers with limited firearm experience, resulting in accidental shootings. Being bitten by a rattlesnake, a common menace throughout much of the West, could prove a death sentence.

Many diseases were contracted along the trail. Children suffered from diphtheria. With primitive sanitary conditions, diarrhea and dysentery were common. Worst of all was cholera. The world experienced a pandemic of cholera in the early 1800s, and by April 1849 the dangerous bacteria proved a killer as far west as Fort Laramie. Illness came suddenly, causing agonizing stomach pains. The victim could appear fine in the morning and was often dead by evening.

Spring thunderstorms on the prairie were unlike storms emigrants had experienced back East. Storms arrived quickly with heavy sheets of rain, continual lightning flashes, and rolling booms of thunder often accompanied by sleet and large hail. Being struck by lightning or falling ill with pneumonia was not uncommon.

Emigrants tended to be overly concerned about the possibility of American Indian attacks, at least in the early years of travel, although most tribes proved more helpful than harmful during this period. Most conflicts with American Indians occurred during the latter years of trail use when traffic had increased and many pioneers decided to homestead rather than continue on to Oregon. American Indian encounters tended to be highly sensationalized in the press, forcing readers to misleadingly conclude that American Indian attacks were a major cause of death on the trail.

6. Register Cliff

On the afternoon following their departure from Fort Laramie, pioneers found a pleasant campground beside the North Platte River. Nearby was a large sandstone bluff rising 100 feet above the valley floor that many of the emigrants viewed as a rock tablet, etching the soft stone with their names, dates, and places of origin. Not surprisingly the bluff became known as **Register Cliff.**

The sandstone cliff is one of the Oregon Trail's best examples of the desire of pioneers to leave a lasting mark of their remarkable journey. While most names represent travel in the 1840s and 1850s, fur traders and mountain men had visited here and left their mark even earlier. The earliest surviving inscription is from July 14,

Inscriptions on Register Cliff where pioneers etched their names in the soft sandstone.

1829, by a French fur trader. A cave along the bottom of the cliff was blasted out to create a storage area for potatoes grown by the land's owner, who operated a ranch here. The site was also the location of a small trading post that later become a Pony Express station.

Wind and water have eroded a considerable number of the historic etchings, and extensive vandalism has obliterated many more. Fortunately for today's travelers the site was gifted to the state of Wyoming in 1932 and is now a state historical park. Fencing has been installed to protect the remaining inscriptions along the far eastern section of the cliff. A walkway and interpretive signs assist today's travelers in understanding this important landmark on the Oregon Trail.

Register Cliff is on the south side of the town of Guernsey. Entering Guernsey on US 26, turn south on South Wyoming Avenue, which becomes South Guernsey Road. Drive past the golf course (is this a surprise, or what?) and follow the road about 2.5 miles to the entrance road to the historic site.

7. Guernsey Ruts

Forced a short distance south of the North Platte River by marshy ground, emigrant wagons fell in line to ascend a soft sandstone hill and create the most impressive ruts along the entirety of the Oregon Trail. The half mile of ruts left by thousands of wagons and the hooves of tens of thousands of draft animals, sometimes appropriately called "Deep Rut Hill," is now part of **Oregon Trail Ruts State Historic Site**.

A paved walking path from the parking area includes information boards and leads to the top of the hill overlooking the ruts. From there visitors can walk east along the narrow passage that has been carved up to 5 feet deep. It is likely heavy freight wagons were a major factor in creating the deep depression, but the amazing ruts create a sense of awe in most who visit here.

In Guernsey turn south off US 26 onto South Wyoming Avenue and drive south through town until crossing the bridge over the North Platte River. Take the first right after the bridge onto Lucinda Rollins Road and drive about a half mile to a road on the left that leads to the parking area.

8. Lucindy Rollins Grave

Not much is known about **Lucindy Rollins,** whose gravestone was not discovered until 1934 near the North Platte River. Her name was legible (although some believed it to be Lucinda, not Lucindy), and a magnifying glass was required to determine June 1849 as the date of death and Dayton, Ohio, the hometown.

After discovery of the stone, articles were placed in newspapers in an attempt to locate a relative. A newspaper article dated May 11, 1934, from the Steamboat Springs, Colorado, paper, the *Steamboat Pilot*, noted the stone's discovery by George O. Houser, the Guernsey newspaper editor, and Fred Burton, and informed readers the Wyoming Historical Landmark Commission had authorized Houser to place the stone in a monument in an "improved plot." Unfortunately, the newspaper notices were unsuccessful in garnering any additional information about Lucindy Rollins.

A location near the North Platte River was chosen for the new gravestone. The cement monument included a glass-covered recessed area that protected the original stone. During the 1960s the monument was vandalized and the original stone was stolen. A plaque dedicated to the pioneer women of Wyoming includes information about Lucindy.

The site is near Oregon Trail Ruts State Historic Site/Guernsey Ruts. When exiting the historic site parking lot, turn left onto Lucinda Rollins Road; the grave is on the right.

9. Warm Springs

A day's travel from Fort Laramie brought many of the pioneers to **Warm Springs,** an unusual natural attraction that some pioneers called the "Emigrants' Laundry Tub." Though only lukewarm, the water was appreciated by weary travelers needing to bathe or wash dust-covered clothes. The warm water and distance from Fort Laramie made this a popular camping spot for the pioneers.

The location actually has two springs, one flowing though a crack in a rim of rock and another bubbling up from a pool. The flow of water sinks out of sight a short distance from the springs.

Warm Springs is located south of Guernsey on land that is part of Camp Guernsey, a National Guard training center headquartered in town. Permission is required to enter the property due to the possibility of military training exercises. Call (307) 836-7810 to request permission.

Warm Springs was a welcome spot where pioneers could bathe and wash clothes. COURTESY OF THE BLM

10. Cold Spring and Rifle Pit Hill

West of present-day Guernsey, emigrants traveling the Oregon Trail used the land around **Cold Spring** as a campground. Nearby, atop a hill to the north, are five V-shaped rifle pits from 18 to 24 inches in depth arranged as a pentagon.

No one is certain what soldiers in the rifle pits would have been protecting. Some believe it was most likely emigrants using the campground or passing nearby along a branch of the Oregon Trail, while others claim it was the stone and limestone quarry about a mile behind the hill. The quarried stone and limestone were used to construct buildings at **Fort Laramie,** 15 miles to the east.

A pull-off on the north side of US 26, about 2 miles west of Guernsey, includes a monument noting the Cold Spring campground and the rifle pits. A large interpretive sign placed by the state of Wyoming describes the possible use of the rifle pits and the importance to emigrants of this and other springs. The rifle pits are not visible from the road, and land behind the monument is private property.

11. Ayres Natural Bridge

Travel along the Oregon Trail was exhausting, and something needed to be extraordinary to lure emigrants into undertaking a side trip. **Courthouse Rock** was one such special landmark that drew many travelers off the trail, but this was to some extent due to emigrants underestimating the distance to reach the monolith.

A landmark nearer the trail that attracted the interest of some emigrants was a picturesque canyon that was home to a 50-foot-high natural bridge. Two miles south of the trail, a brilliant red rock gorge houses a large limestone arch that spans spring-fed La Prele Creek. To access the canyon and enjoy the creek's cool waters, emigrants were required to descend a steep 30-foot rock wall and struggle through dense thicket.

According to legend, a young brave had been struck by lightning and killed here, resulting in local tribes believing an evil spirit resided in the canyon. White settlers who learned of the legend began using the canyon as a shelter from American Indian attacks. Members of the Donner party visited the landmark in 1846, and William Henry Jackson photographed the natural bridge in 1870.

The land on which the natural bridge is located was gifted in 1919 to Converse County by the Ayres family, which ranched along La Prele Creek. It is now part of a county park that includes an attractive picnic area and small campground. Having visited the site for the first time in 2021, we can attest that it is one of the most idyllic locations along the entirety of the Oregon Trail.

The Team of John C. Fremont and Kit Carson

A chance meeting between US Army engineer **John C. Fremont** and frontiersman **Kit Carson** birthed a partnership that would have a profound effect on expansion of the American West.

Georgia-born Fremont had been educated in science and worked as a mathematics instructor aboard a US Navy ship before becoming an assistant engineer on a railroad survey team and a civil engineer in the Army Topographical Corps of Engineers. Fremont gained extensive knowledge in geology and topography while surveying and mapping the upper Mississippi and Missouri Rivers. Kentucky-born Kit Carson, 4 years older than Fremont, grew up in Missouri and at age 15 ran away from home to join traders headed to Santa Fe. Carson became an experienced hunter and trapper while exploring the West.

In 1842 Fremont was assigned by the US Army to map the Oregon Trail to the Rocky Mountains. During a steamboat ride on the Missouri River to start the trip, he encoun-

Kit Carson and John C. Fremont met during a steamboat ride and subsequently worked together mapping the West. PUBLIC DOMAIN

tered Kit Carson, who, following 8 years hunting and trapping in the West, had returned to his Missouri home for a family visit. Finding that both his parents had died and the homestead was in ruins, he traveled to St. Louis and boarded the steamboat to head back West.

During their meeting Fremont asked Carson to guide his expedition along the Oregon Trail. The two men subsequently spent 5 months traveling, writing, and mapping the land. Fremont included mention of Carson in his final reports, and both explorers gained considerable fame when the guidebook, maps, and other information appeared in many newspapers.

Carson accompanied Fremont's second 1843–1844 expedition with an assignment to map the remainder of the Oregon Trail. During a fourteen-month trip the expedition also explored present-day Utah and California. Following publication of this second report, Fremont became known as the "Pathfinder" and Carson earned his status as a Western hero.

Their final expedition together in 1845 had more of a political flavor, as it was designed to assist President Polk wrest control of California from Mexico. While in California they engaged in skirmishes with American Indians but were successful in providing the president with information that helped him acquire California.

John Fremont and Kit Carson were an effective team: Carson was instrumental in leading the expeditions and helping expedition members survive in the wilderness; Fremont was the expert on describing the territory and, with help from cartographer Charles Preuss, developing intricate maps. Their complementary skills brought fame to each.

Ayres Natural Bridge west of Douglas was not on the trail, but some emigrants hiked to visit the site.

Approximately 12 miles west of Douglas on I-25, take exit 151 and head south on CR 13 for 5 miles to where the road enters the park. Watch for cattle that consider the county road part of their pasture.

12. Ada Magill Grave

Caleb and Nancy Magill, along with their children, departed Kansas and headed to Oregon in June 1864. Their youngest, Ada, grew ill while the family was camping near Fort Laramie. The 3-year-old appeared to be recovering and the family continued west, but the illness returned and the youngster died near today's town of Glenrock. According to her father, Ada was buried near the trail in a casket constructed from boards of an old wagon. Her grave was then covered with rocks to protect the remains from animals. Following the burial the family continued west and settled near Portland.

In the early 1900s it was determined the grave was in the path of a proposed road, resulting in Ada's remains being moved 30 feet to the north. A new headstone was inscribed with the same words as the original.

From US 20/26, about 5.2 miles west of Glenrock, turn north at the brown sign for "Big Muddy Bridge Public Access." Turn right onto the first gravel road (prior to crossing the bridge) and drive about a quarter mile. The grave sits on the north side of the road near the crossing of an old railroad track.

13. Reshaw's Bridge

The **Mormon Ferry** had been operating along the North Platte River west of today's Casper for several years when trader **Jean "John" Baptiste Richard** and four partners decided in fall 1852 to construct a bridge about 3 miles to the east. Other ferries were also operating in the area. The span required about a year to complete and became known as **Reshaw's Bridge.** Richard's French accent caused his name to be interpreted by emigrants as "Reshaw."

The bridge foundation was constructed of diamond-shaped timber piers filled with stone. Spaced at intervals of 30 to 40 feet, the piers were connected with large logs over which was laid a floor of thick wood planks. A railing was added to each side. By one estimate the finished bridge was about 830 feet in length and 18 feet wide. The charge for crossing depended on the height and swiftness of the river current, with the highest fee being $8 per wagon. A trading post and blacksmith shop were established at the site.

A replica of a section of Reshaw's Bridge is northeast of Casper.

Business was brisk with freighters crossing both directions, and the new bridge soon ran the nearby Mormons out of the transportation business. In 1860 much of the bridge traffic was diverted to a new bridge built by Richard's onetime partner, Louis Guinard, near the Mormon Ferry site.

By 1865 Richard had sold the entirety of his operations and departed the area. The following winter soldiers from Fort Caspar dismantled Reshaw's Bridge and used the wood as building materials and firewood.

A replica of one section of the bridge and an interpretive plaque are near the original site northeast of Casper in the town of Evansville. To reach the park, take exit 182 off I-25 (or US 26) and head north on Curtis Road, which becomes Cemetery Road. Just prior to reaching the river, turn left on Platte Park Road. Reshaw Park is on the right.

14. Mormon Ferry

River crossings were often a dangerous undertaking for emigrants on the trail, especially during the spring and early summer when rivers were high and fast flowing. Many wagon trains following the south side of the North Platte River chose to cross to the north side near present-day Casper, where the river was 100 to 300 yards wide and up to 10 to 15 feet deep in places.

A replica of the original Mormon Ferry and a section of the Louis Guinard Bridge are on the grounds of the Fort Caspar Museum.

Traveling west in 1847, the first group of Mormon pioneers, which included **Brigham Young,** crossed here on their way to the Salt Lake Valley. They first floated some wagon boxes across before trying rafts. The men finally constructed a ferry using cottonwood dugout canoes with pine poles for decking. More than one hundred wagons were waiting to cross by the time the work was completed.

Brigham Young saw that money could be made assisting emigrants in crossing the river, so in the spirit of religious capitalism he selected nine members of the group to remain behind and operate a ferry business. In subsequent years church members returned from the Salt Lake Valley to operate the ferry during high season.

The ferry proved to be a rewarding operation for the Mormons. So good, in fact, that by 1850, competing ferries were jostling for the emigrants' business. The Mormons decided to exit the ferry business following the 1852 season when John Richard and his partners commenced construction of a substantial bridge over the North Platte.

A replica of the ferry is located on the grounds of the Fort Caspar Museum. Phone (307) 235-8462 for information. The museum is located at 4001 Fort Caspar Road in Casper. From I-25 take exit 188B and drive south to 13th Street. At 13th, turn right into the museum parking lot.

15. Guinard Bridge

Six miles upstream from Reshaw's Bridge, a competing bridge was being constructed in 1859 by Richard's former partner, Louis Guinard. After completion the new structure became known as the **Guinard Bridge,** or the Upper Platte Bridge, while Reshaw's Bridge then became the Lower Platte Bridge.

In 1862 the US Army established a military post at the crossing to protect the telegraph. Initially called Platte Bridge Station, the post's name was changed in 1865 to Fort Casper in honor of Lieutenant Caspar Collins, who in 1865 was killed by the Cheyenne, Arapaho, and Lakota near Platte Bridge Station. (Officials unfortunately misspelled the lieutenant's name.)

A replica of a section of the Guinard Bridge sits beside a replica of the Mormon Ferry near the actual locations on the grounds of Fort Caspar Museum. A plaque beside the replicas indicates that the centerpiece of the Platte Bridge Station and Fort Caspar was the bridge built here by Louis Guinard in 1859–1860 and used until Fort Caspar was abandoned in 1867. The bridge superstructure stood on twenty-eight timber cribbings filled with rock and gravel. The bridge was 17 feet wide and just over 1,000 feet long. Construction cost was estimated at $40,000, and the toll for wagon crossings was $1 to $6, depending on the height of the river. An additional toll was charged for animals and people.

See the Mormon Ferry entry for directions to the Guinard Bridge.

Father Pierre-Jean De Smet: Jesuit Missionary to the West

Father Pierre-Jean De Smet first headed west in 1840 with a fur trading caravan. LIBRARY OF CONGRESS

In 1821 **Pierre-Jean De Smet** left a Catholic seminary in Belgium and traveled to the United States. At age 20, the future Jesuit priest wanted to become a missionary to American Indian tribes in the West. Little did he know at the time he would become one of the Oregon Trail's most influential individuals. De Smet continued his studies in Maryland and then St. Louis, where he was ordained. The priest first established a school for Osage boys near St. Louis and several years later a mission in Iowa Territory for the Potawatomie. Although veiled as benevolent institutions to educate American Indian children, the schools were formed to Christianize the children and strip them of their culture. They were effectively isolated from their families and forbidden from speaking any Indigenous languages.

At the request of the Flathead tribe, Father De Smet was sent to the far West for the first time in 1840. Traveling along what would become the Oregon Trail with a fur company caravan heading for a rendezvous in the Rocky Mountains, the priest had been asked to evaluate the possibility of establishing a mission for the Flatheads. The following year, with five priests in tow, De Smet joined with the Bidwell-Bartleson group, which would become the first emigrants to attempt a wagon crossing from Missouri to California. According to plan the priests split from the main group in today's Soda Springs, Idaho, and continued with a group going to Oregon. Reaching Fort Hall, the priests left the Oregon-bound emigrants and headed to what is now western Montana's Bitterroot Valley, where they established the first of several Jesuit missions for American Indians in the Northwest.

The missions were not self-supporting, and their maintenance required that Father De Smet make journeys back East in addition to several European trips to secure supplies and funds and recruit additional missionaries.

As a result of the forcible removal of American Indian children from their families and tribal land and the federally funded assimilation into Anglo culture, the situation between white settlers and American Indian tribes worsened greatly by the 1860s. Father De Smet worked with the federal government in attempt to mediate peace between the tribes and settlers. He continued to raise money for the missions in the West until his death in 1873.

16. Fort Caspar

The Guinard Bridge spanning the North Platte River attracted considerable emigrant traffic after its completion in 1859. The increase in traffic, in turn, resulted in the construction of a complex of buildings including a trading post, an Overland Stage Company stop, and a Pony Express relay station.

In an effort to protect the emigrants, the mail service, and the transcontinental telegraph lines, the latter having been completed in 1861, the US Army constructed a series of forts along the emigrant trails. In 1862 a company of soldiers sent to the Guinard Bridge named their new garrison Platte Bridge Station.

In July 1865 **Lieutenant Caspar Collins** led soldiers to meet an army supply train that it would escort back to the fort. Soon after their departure the group was ambushed by Lakota Sioux, Cheyenne, and Arapaho warriors, and Collins, along with four other soldiers, were killed in what became known as the Battle of Platte Bridge.

Additional troops soon arrived at Platte Bridge Station with the charge to expand the fort to accommodate a larger force. The expanded fort was renamed Fort Casper (Collins's name was misspelled). Collins's first name was used due to an existing fort previously named for his father.

By fall the transcontinental railroad had reached Cheyenne and the telegraph line had been rerouted, resulting in a government order that Fort Casper close down with "troops and all useful materials, including buildings, transferred to Fort Fetterman."

A replica of Fort Casper was constructed in 1936 as a project of the Works Progress Administration (WPA). Building furnishings are as they would have been in 1865. At completion the fort's name was changed to correct the initial spelling error. The fort is on the grounds of the **Fort Caspar Museum,** located at 4001 Fort Caspar Road in Casper. From I-25 take exit 188B and drive south to 13th Street, then turn right into the fort. Phone (307) 235-8462 for information.

A replica of Fort Caspar, the original of which was abandoned in 1867, is located beside the Fort Caspar Museum.

17. Bessemer Bend

West of present-day Casper, the North Platte River makes a sharp bend to the south toward its headwaters in the Rocky Mountains. For pioneers following the river's south bank, this was their final chance to cross to the north side and head southwest toward Independence Rock, the Sweetwater River, and South Pass. The North Platte, which could be a bear to cross during the late spring, was generally easier to ford by July when the majority of pioneers arrived.

The primary crossing point in the early years of the trail was at **Bessemer Bend** (also called Red Buttes Crossing), near the red sandstone buttes that gave the crossing its early name. By 1847 toll bridges and ferries were available east of Red Buttes, although some pioneers continued to ford here to avoid the toll required of the easier crossings to the east. The route ahead to the Sweetwater River would be a rough one, and pioneers often chose to enjoy some time here where they had clean water, grass for livestock, and some beautiful vistas.

The crossing site is now part of **Bessemer Bend National Historic Site.** A Bureau of Land Management interpretive area offers displays, a picnic area, and vault toilets. The site is approximately 13 miles southwest of Casper via WY 220. After milepost 106 look for a Bessemer Bend National Historic Site sign and turn right on CR 308.

18–20. Wyoming's County Road 319: An Exceptional Drive along the Oregon Trail

County Road 319 is an excellent driving experience along the Oregon Trail. The rural dirt road offers access to memorable landmarks and pristine pioneer swales. Vehicle

Red Buttes Crossing at Bessemer Bend was the last place for pioneers to ford the North Platte River.

traffic is minimal, and the scenery highlights Wyoming's wide-open spaces. The road is slow, rough, and can be dusty, but this only puts the traveler in a frame of mind to better appreciate what the pioneers encountered during a significant portion of their six-month journey.

From Bessemer Bend (see driving directions to the site in the Bessemer Bend entry) turn right onto CR 308, which angles west. Continue on CR 308 until intersecting CR 319 and turn left. Now begins a 31-mile stretch near the historic trail. Mileage shown at each site is from Bessemer Bend. Take your time because there is a lot to savor along the way. The road ends at WY 220 where travelers can turn east (left) and return to Casper or turn west (right) and drive a short distance to Independence Rock. *Warning:* It is advisable to avoid the county road during wet weather.

18. Rock Avenue (11.3 miles)

Rock Avenue is a jagged row of sharp shale and sandstone rocks that forced emigrant wagon trains along a narrow and steep downhill path toward Willow Springs. With the appearance of the serrated back of an ancient reptile, the landmark went by a variety of names including Devil's Backbone, Rock Lane, and Avenue of Rocks. The formation is particularly impressive because it juts out from a rolling landscape of rangeland.

Numerous pioneers etched their names on the rocks here, but most have been lost to natural erosion and road construction. Some remain, however, and this is a worthwhile place to park your vehicle and enjoy some time exploring an unusual Oregon Trail landmark.

Rock Avenue is an unusual landmark on the Oregon-California Trail west of Casper.

A present-day cowboy herding bulls near Willow Spring.

19. Willow Spring (17.2 miles)

After crossing the North Platte River near present-day Casper, the pioneers and their livestock had been without palatable water for 2 days before arriving at **Willow Spring,** an oasis in the high desert of today's central Wyoming. The location offered good drinking water, grass for livestock, and cottonwood trees for shade and firewood.

With the discovery of gold in California, the oasis of Willow Spring morphed into more of a quagmire by 1850, when arriving pioneers discovered its trees cut and most of the grass already consumed by livestock of earlier arrivals.

All that remains today at the spring are parched remnants of a dead cottonwood tree along with a large patch of vegetation fed by a depleted spring. An interpretive marker offers an overview of the spring.

20. Prospect Hill (21 miles)

Near the far side of Willow Spring the pioneers encountered **Prospect Hill,** a steep grade that rewarded the travelers with an outstanding view of the countryside below and around them. Today's visitors enjoy the same viewpoint, little changed from the vista that captivated the pioneers. The Bureau of Land Management has a viewing area with exhibits. Wagon swales of the old trail are identified with markers.

Independence Rock was a popular stop where pioneers etched their names in the massive granite rock.

21. Independence Rock

One of the Oregon Trail's best-known landmarks is a massive granite rock given the name "The Great Register of the Desert" by Father Pierre-Jean De Smet during an 1840 stopover on the way to the Bitterroot area of Montana. Father De Smet's designation resulted from the many names and dates he discovered etched and painted by the numerous mountain men and pioneers who had paused here before him. The rock became a guest register for nearly every well-known trail guide, fur trader, and pioneer who passed by including John Fremont, the Sublette brothers, Nathaniel

A view overlooking the Sweetwater River from the top of Independence Rock.

Wyeth, Captain James Bonneville, and Thomas "Broken Hand" Fitzpatrick. Wyoming State Parks estimates that at one time over 5,000 names adorned the rock. Unfortunately, many have been lost to rain and wind.

One of those early mountain men passing though was William Sublette, who in 1830 was leading a supply wagon caravan when he and his men celebrated the Fourth of July while camped here. From that point forward the giant granite landmark was generally known as **Independence Rock.** Although Sublette's group was headed to an annual rendezvous, the location became thought of as a destination pioneers should reach by July 4 in order to avoid winter conditions in the mountains that would be encountered farther west.

Independence Rock rises to 137 feet with a circumference of over 1 mile and was described by some early visitors as having the appearance of a stone turtle or beached whale. The rock sits beside the Sweetwater River, which pioneers followed to reach the Continental Divide at South Pass. The giant rock, being near water and grass for livestock, made the area a popular resting spot for pioneer wagon trains.

Independence Rock State Historic Site is about 55 miles southwest of Casper via WY 220. A path from the parking area leads across a footbridge above visible wagon swales to the west side of the rock, which is encircled by a 1-mile walking path. Visitors are free to climb the rock to search out remaining pioneer etchings while enjoying outstanding views of the surrounding landscape.

22. Devil's Gate

Departing Independence Rock, the pioneers followed the Sweetwater River southwest. Five miles down the trail, about where the Sweetwater turns and starts wiggling its way east toward the North Platte, another granite landmark caught the emigrants' attention. While not directly on the trail, **Devil's Gate** offered such an unusual sight that numerous travelers decided to take a closer look. Upon their arrival many etched their names just as they had at Independence Rock.

Devil's Gate is a massive V-shaped cut in a granite ridge resulting from millions of years of erosion by the Sweetwater River. The name's origin is unclear, although many believe it is connected with several murders and other deaths that are thought to have taken place here.

It would seem the river should have been smarter and, like the pioneers, taken a less onerous route around rather than through the ridge. The Sweetwater established its path millions of years ago at a time when the region was filled with sediment and volcanic ash. By the time the stream of water had cut through the sediment and reached granite, the river's path was set and the water's cutting continued, producing today's impressive cleft.

Trail Heartbreak: The Mormon Handcart Tragedy

More than 1,000 converted Mormon emigrants from Britain and Scandinavia commenced travel from Florence, Nebraska (now part of Omaha) to Salt Lake City in August 1856. Pioneers typically started their trips in May, late enough to ensure grass for livestock but early enough to cross the high country before winter arrived. An August departure was a risky choice that, combined with bad luck, proved to be a costly mistake.

By 1856 Mormon officials were short of funds and told emigrants to travel to Utah with handcarts rather than using wagons pulled by draft animals that Brigham Young considered too expensive and slow. The carts were shallow wooden boxes 4 feet in length and 3 feet wide perched on a single wooden axle connecting two large wooden wheels. They were built and powered by the emigrants who pushed or pulled their possessions to Utah. No one said this would be an easy trip.

Several companies had successfully completed the trip to Utah earlier in 1856, but the last two companies to depart, Willie Company on August 17 and Martin Company on August 27, encountered severe winter weather in Wyoming. In mid-October both companies, by then short of supplies, were halted by a blizzard. Brigham Young had learned from travelers arriving earlier of the late arrivals and dispatched rescue personnel with supplies to assist the stranded emigrants.

Rescuers were able to reach and help both companies, although not before many exhausted emigrants expired from cold and lack of food. More would die during the remaining trek to Utah. A rescue party helped Martin Company reach shelter near Devil's Gate where the emigrants camped in a small cove for several days. Both companies finally reached Salt Lake City in November.

Desiring to tell the story of emigrant handcart travel to Salt Lake City, in 1997 the Mormon Church acquired ownership of 13,000 acres near Devil's Gate from owners of the Sun Ranch. In addition they signed a lease agreement with the Bureau of Land Management for Martin's Cove, where the Martin Company sheltered in 1856. A ranch house has been converted into a visitor center containing artwork and artifacts. A 5-mile (round-trip) hiking trail leads to the cove, with handcarts available to push or pull a portion of the way. A separate 1-mile (round-trip) trail offers access to the Sweetwater River and Devil's Gate through which it flows.

The **Mormon Handcart Historic Site** is just off WY 220, about three-quarters of a mile west of the BLM pullout for Devil's Gate. Admission to the visitor center is free. Phone (307) 328-2953 for information.

The cut through the rock is about 370 feet deep and over a quarter mile long. The nearly 300-foot width at the top is ten times that of the bottom, making the path through the granite too narrow to have allowed wagons to pass alongside the river. Thus the historic trail looped south around Devil's Gate and caught up with the Sweetwater.

Devil's Gate is quite impressive both at a distance while driving along WY 220 and up close. For the latter, visit the Mormon Handcart Historic Site at 47600 W. Hwy. 220. A mile-long round-trip walking trail leads from the visitor center's parking lot to the river.

23. Split Rock

Split Rock is the westernmost of three large granite landmarks (the others being Independence Rock and Devil's Gate) observed by pioneers as they traversed the Sweetwater Valley. Although not directly on the Oregon Trail, the location and 1,000-foot height above the surrounding landscape allowed the emigrants to utilize Split Rock as a navigational device that pointed them toward the Continental Divide at South Pass. The landmark could be seen when the pioneers departed Devil's Gate and would linger in sight for yet another day after they passed by to the south.

The prominent notch or cleft, sometimes compared to a gunsight, resulted from the erosion of fractures in the granite. Although difficult to imagine, these prominent granite rocks were once part of a mountain range that sank and became covered by thousands of feet of sand and, later, a large shallow lake.

Heading south on WY 220 from Devil's Gate, turn right (west) on US 287 and drive about 8 miles to a pullout on the right with a BLM interpretive sign. Just over 3 miles farther down the road is another pullout with an interpretive monument and better view of Split Rock.

Although off the main trail, Split Rock was used by pioneers as a navigational aid as they moved toward South Pass.

24. Ice Slough

Pioneers following the Sweetwater River on their way to the Continental Divide at South Pass came across a welcome gift of nature. As a preview of other natural wonders they would come across later in the trip at Soda Springs, the emigrants discovered a field of ice during the early summer. Actually, the ice was underground, but not so deep they couldn't dig a little and recover ice that could be used to cool drinking water carried in barrels on their wagons.

Referred to as "Ice Spring" at the time, a tributary of the Sweetwater essentially watered a meadow covered with insulating vegetation. The peat-like vegetation provided protection during the spring and a portion of the summer for water that had frozen during the harsh winter. According to pioneer journals, the ice could be collected by using a spade or axe to dig a foot or so into the vegetation. While water atop the ice was alkaline, the ice itself was clear and free of bad taste. Later in the summer the underground ice melted and mixed with the alkaline water. Irrigation and climate change have resulted in the slough now being mostly dry and covered with different vegetation from when pioneer wagons rolled through.

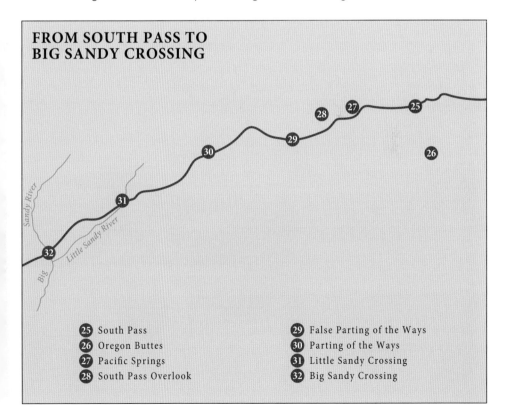

FROM SOUTH PASS TO BIG SANDY CROSSING

25 South Pass
26 Oregon Buttes
27 Pacific Springs
28 South Pass Overlook
29 False Parting of the Ways
30 Parting of the Ways
31 Little Sandy Crossing
32 Big Sandy Crossing

A pullout for the slough is on US 287, 9.5 miles south of Jeffrey City. A large interpretive board offers information about the ice slough, which is east of the highway and on private property.

25. South Pass

In 1805 Lewis and Clark's Corps of Discovery nearly perished searching for an accessible path through the Rocky Mountains. Seven years later, fur trader **John Stuart,** on a mission to carry important papers from Fort Astoria at the mouth of the Columbia River to John Jacob Astor in New York, was offered advice by a Shoshone regarding an easier path through the mountains. On October 22, 1812, Stuart and six companions crossed a "low gap" that was to become the magical key for unlocking the door to emigrant wagon trains heading west.

South Pass, named to differentiate it from the northern crossing used by Lewis and Clark, became a 20-mile-wide saddle across the Continental Divide for travelers on the Oregon, California, and Mormon Trails, along with the Pony Express and transcontinental telegraph line. There is no more important landmark along the entire trail than South Pass.

The incline leading to the 7,412-foot pass actually started near Independence Rock when pioneers began following the Sweetwater River. The grade near the pass proved so gradual that many pioneers didn't realize they had crossed to the west of the Continental Divide until arriving at Pacific Springs, where they observed water flowing west rather than east.

The monument to Narcissa Whitman and Eliza Spalding on the distant hill is approximately where pioneers crossed the Continental Divide at South Pass.

Monument to Narcissa Whitman and Eliza Spalding, the first white women known to cross South Pass.

While Stuart told others of South Pass upon returning to the East, the first wagons didn't utilize the pass until Captain Benjamin Bonneville led a caravan of twenty freight wagons across the divide in 1832. Missionary Marcus Whitman and his new bride, Narcissa, crossed South Pass 4 years later. By the 1840s the pass was in regular use by pioneers headed to Oregon, California, Montana, and the Salt Lake Valley.

No other landmark on the Oregon Trail can offer the magical experience of standing in the ghostly silence of South Pass. With the Wind River Range to the north and Oregon Buttes to the south, the connection with the pioneers is surreal. This is the place! This is where several hundred thousand pioneers successfully crossed America's spine, and the view today is little changed from the 1840s when they did it.

From the South Pass Rest Area on WY 28, drive 0.9 mile south and turn east on Oregon Buttes Road. Drive 2.8 miles on this good-quality gravel road until reaching the two-track road of deep ruts and turn right. This is the original Oregon Trail. About three-quarters of a mile down this trail near a cattle guard are a BLM interpretive exhibit and two iconic markers, one honoring Narcissa Whitman and Eliza Spalding for being the first white women to cross the pass. A nearby monument placed by Ezra Meeker marks the trail.

Oregon Buttes served as an important landmark for pioneers as they crossed South Pass into Oregon Country.

26. Oregon Buttes

Oregon Buttes served as an important landmark for pioneers crossing the Continental Divide at South Pass. The two flat buttes plus a nearby conical butte rise out of the desert to an elevation of 8,612 feet, and offered an approximate guide to pioneers crossing into Oregon Country. This part of the continent was acquired by the United States in 1846 under a treaty with Britain. Prior to this, the early pioneers were entering a land that was jointly held by the United States and Britain.

The road to the buttes isn't as bad as you might expect, although no interpretive signs are nearby once you arrive. This trail landmark can be easily seen from both South Pass and South Pass Overlook.

27. Pacific Springs

A few miles after crossing the Continental Divide at South Pass, pioneers arrived at **Pacific Springs,** a sea of green in an otherwise austere land of colorless dirt, sand, and rocks. The springs offered water to drink and, at least early in the season, feed for livestock. Drinkable water and vegetation weren't as plentiful for late-arriving wagon trains in 1849, when trail traffic was heavy with travelers headed to the California goldfields. Water from the springs drained west, evidence to the pioneers that they had crossed the peak of the Rocky Mountains.

While Pacific Springs may not produce as much water as in the mid-1800s, it continues to offer sufficient dampness for vegetation to color the large depression below South Pass. During our own visit we had to maneuver our vehicle through a group of cattle that considered it their property and viewed us as an unwanted distraction.

Ezra Meeker: Public Face of the Oregon Trail

Ezra Meeker, together with his wife, Eliza, and their 7-week-old son, in 1852 headed west from Iowa in a covered wagon. Joining other pioneers, the family spent 5 months traveling to Oregon Territory where they eventually settled in the Puyallup Valley of present-day Washington.

Meeker tried his hand at several enterprises, including selling provisions to Canadian gold miners, but struck it rich in the mid-1860s growing hops used in brewing beer. This ended badly in 1892 when his crops were devastated by an infestation of hop aphids.

After settling in the Northwest, Meeker had become an avid promoter of the region and in 1870 authored *Washington Territory West of the Cascades*, an eighty-page pamphlet he took to New York to sell. There he met Jay Cook, a financier involved with the Northern Pacific Railroad. Cook purchased all the pamphlets and compensated Meeker to travel throughout New England promoting the Northwest.

Ezra Meeker spent much of his later years attempting to popularize and preserve the Oregon Trail. LIBRARY OF CONGRESS

Wanting to preserve the legacy of the westward movement over the Oregon Trail, Meeker committed to having the trail marked and protected. In 1906, at age 76, he retraced the route, this time traveling west to east in a covered wagon pulled by two oxen. Stopping along the way, the old pioneer presented talks about the trail while requesting donations for an Oregon Trail marker to be placed in each city and at major trail landmarks along the way. As markers he chose large rocks engraved with "Oregon Trail 1842–1857," which became known as "Meeker Markers." The trip ended in Washington, D.C., where Meeker met with President Theodore Roosevelt.

Meeker became well-known during additional trips following the trail. His next trip by covered wagon occurred in 1910. Five years later he drove an automobile with his wagon cover mounted atop the car. In 1924 he capped his travels by flying over the trail in an open cockpit biplane. Meeker became ill while preparing for a 1928 trip and passed away just short of his 98th birthday.

Ezra and Eliza Meeker's 1887 mansion in Puyallup, Washington, is now owned by the Ezra Meeker Historical Society and open to the public during designated hours. For information call (253) 697-9468.

The noted landmark can be accessed by continuing to follow the two-track road at South Pass that leads west to South Pass Overlook and WY 28. Somewhat easier and shorter access is available by starting from the overlook on WY 28 and taking the dirt road that leads to the springs. See South Pass Overlook for directions.

28. South Pass Overlook

The Bureau of Land Management has constructed an excellent overlook with views of several of the historic trail's best-known landmarks. A paved path leads past five interpretive signs that present an overview of the fur trade, Oregon Buttes, death on the trail, Twin Mounds, and South Pass. Best of all are the outstanding views of South Pass, Pacific Springs, Oregon Buttes, and Twin Mounds. A rugged dirt road from the overlook leads to Pacific Springs and South Pass, but don't try it unless you are driving a high-clearance vehicle.

The overlook is on the east side of WY 28, 5.3 miles southwest of the South Pass Rest Area.

29. False Parting of the Ways

A modern-day curiosity along the Oregon Trail has become a popular stop for travelers following the historic trail through Wyoming. An attractive granite trail marker with misleading information was erected in 1956 by the Historic Landmark Commission of

The roadside monument states it is for Parting of the Ways, but it is actually the False Parting of the Ways.

Wyoming. The marker, a short distance off WY 28, designates the site as the famed Parting of the Ways in which the Sublette Cutoff forked west off the main trail and headed for the Bear River and Fort Hall in today's Idaho, while the main trail continued southwest to Fort Bridger.

The true Parting of the Ways is another 9.5 miles west and relatively difficult to access. The incorrect Historic Landmark Commission marker is actually where the Oregon Trail intersects the Point of Rocks to South Pass Stage Route. Despite the misleading marker, this is a worthwhile stop with excellent swales no matter where they may lead.

The monument is accessed from along a short side road and parking area that parallels the north side of WY 28, 5.5 miles southwest of South Pass Overlook.

30. Parting of the Ways

Parting of the Ways during the era of historic trail travel referred to the intentional separation of pioneers who had been traveling together, often for months. When parting, most emigrants didn't know if they would ever see one another again. Parting of the Ways near South Pass in Wyoming is where the Sublette Cutoff separates

True Parting of the Ways. The left fork heads up toward Little Sandy Crossing and Fort Bridger. The right is the Sublette Cutoff that leads west to the Green River. COURTESY OF BLM

Trail Cutoffs: Finding a Better Route

American Indians, explorers, mountain men, and traders were continually in search of new routes that would save time or bypass obstacles. These might entail shortcuts or routes that avoided steep grades and river crossings. Emigrants following the Oregon Trail were no different. Pioneers wanted to arrive in Oregon as quickly, easily, and safely as possible. These altered routes didn't always come without a cost. A cutoff that provided a shorter path might include a lengthy stretch without water or grass. A new route that offered a safer passage might require additional days of travel.

Over the years a series of improvements and altered routes significantly reduced the time required by pioneers to reach Oregon's Willamette Valley. They also reduced the risk. Rafts were constructed, bridges were built, trading posts popped up, military presence increased, and shortcuts were blazed. Four primary Oregon Trail cutoffs include:

Sublette, or **Greenwood Cutoff**—Caleb Greenwood promoted a trail in present-day Wyoming that eliminated a relatively lengthy dip from South Pass to Fort Bridger before heading back north. Initially blazed by William Sublette in the 1820s, it is best known as the Sublette Cutoff. The route headed west from about 18 miles south of South Pass to rejoin the main trail just short of where it entered present-day Idaho. The cutoff saved about 3 days but required 45 miles of travel without firewood, grass, or water. The Sublette Cutoff opened in 1844 and proved quite popular.

Goodale Cutoff—In 1852 a Shoshone migration trail was promoted by John Jeffrey to generate business for the ferry he built at the mouth of the Blackfoot River northwest of Fort Hall. The new route enjoyed little success until 1862 when emigrants on the main trail that followed the south bank of the Snake River faced American Indian hostilities. Concern of potential conflict caused the majority of pioneers to begin choosing this 230-mile route, known later as the Goodale Cutoff. The route was pretty much a straight line from Fort Hall to Fort Boise. On

from the main trail by heading west toward the Bear River and Fort Hall, while the main trail continues southwest to Fort Bridger. This latter fork was taken by those headed to California and the Salt Lake Valley, and also by many emigrants going to Oregon.

The **Sublette Cutoff,** explored by Caleb Greenwood and Isaac Hitchcock in 1844, saved pioneers 45 miles and 3 days of travel by avoiding the trip to Fort Bridger. The major drawback was the cutoff route traversed the Little Colorado Desert, which was hot, dusty, and offered no water, with little for the animals to eat other than sagebrush.

It was a difficult decision for some, but those who needed provisions or were concerned about the condition of their livestock generally avoided the cutoff and headed to Fort Bridger. The cutoff became quite popular in 1849 when most travelers were in a rush to get to the California goldfields.

The true Parting of the Ways is difficult to access for most of today's travelers. We know because we tried but threw in the towel as the dirt road from Little Sandy

the downside, it was a difficult, hot route that passed through a corner of today's Craters of the Moon National Monument. The cutoff also resulted in slow progress due to wagons needing to travel single file around the crooked edges of lava flows.

Lander Trail—Engineer Frederick Lander designed a 229-mile trail for the Department of the Interior that connected South Pass with Soda Springs in today's Idaho. It opened in 1859 and saved pioneers about 80 miles and 7 days of travel. The road, primarily for pioneers headed to California, cut across three mountain ranges, had seven bridges, and was completed in 3 months at a cost of $70,000. It was steep and rough but offered timber, water, and grass.

Hudspeth's Cutoff—When gold was discovered in California, tens of thousands of individuals hoping for quick riches headed west to the goldfields wanting to stake a claim as quickly as possible. Benoni M. Hudspeth and John J. Myers, two well-traveled mountain men, blazed what became known as Hudspeth's Cutoff, which parted from the Oregon Trail just past present-day Soda Springs. The cutoff headed west and rejoined the main California Trail northeast of City of Rocks. The route saved travelers about 25 miles but proved a difficult journey across four mountainous regions.

Other cutoffs of note include the **Applegate Trail,** which headed southwest from Fort Hall and followed the Humboldt River before turning northwest to approach the Willamette Valley from the south. The **Childs Cutoff** departed Fort Laramie on the north bank of the North Platte River, allowing pioneers to avoid crossing the river near present-day Casper. The **Barlow Road** allowed pioneers to avoid the dangers of ferrying the Columbia River by heading south out of The Dalles, going around the south shoulder of Mount Hood, and traveling west to Oregon City. The **Seminoe Cutoff** was a 35-mile trail south of the main trail in today's Wyoming that avoided multiple crossings of the Sweetwater River.

Crossing continued to deteriorate the farther we drove. The parting is more easily reached from WY 28 to the east, but the drive is still difficult, and getting hung up in this remote country isn't a pleasant experience. An additional issue is the possibility of taking a wrong turn on one or more of the intersecting dirt roads after leaving the main highway. For most, it is probably wise to be satisfied with the knowledge the true parting wasn't far away while standing by the monument at False Parting of the Ways.

31. Little Sandy Crossing

The Little Sandy begins its journey on the western slopes of the Wind River Range and flows southwest to become a tributary of the Big Sandy River. More creek than river, it represented yet another stream for the pioneers to cross regardless of the path they had chosen at Parting of the Ways.

The wandering creek offered pioneers the first good water since crossing the Continental Divide at South Pass with a stop at Pacific Springs. Wagon trains often chose to spend the night near **Little Sandy Crossing.** In 1846 the ill-fated George Donner was elected captain of his group near the crossing. A year later it was here that famed mountain man Jim Bridger met Brigham Young and offered the newcomer some negative thoughts about attempting to raise crops in the Salt Lake Valley.

From the BLM South Pass Overlook, drive about 24.5 miles southwest on WY 28 and turn right on Farson 4th East Road where you see a large, brown metal barn. Drive about 4 miles on the gravel road and turn right at the sign for the crossing. Cross two cattle guards and park near the bridge over the Little Sandy. A BLM interpretive sign is nearby.

32. Big Sandy Crossing

A little over 8 miles after crossing Little Sandy River, emigrants traveling southwest toward Fort Bridger met the Little Sandy's more significant brother, the **Big Sandy River.** They would cross and then follow the Big Sandy toward Fort Bridger for 25 miles to where it emptied into the Green River. The crossing point for the Big Sandy was also the site of a Pony Express and Overland Stage station.

Pioneers choosing to follow the Sublette Cutoff toward Fort Hall were also required to cross the Big Sandy, but at a different location to the west. Along this route the river would be their last access to water for 45 miles along a route that was shorter, but more difficult and dangerous.

The Donner Party camped at Big Sandy Crossing on July 24, 1846.

The pioneer river crossing on the main trail toward Fort Bridger is beneath the modern bridge that now spans the Big Sandy on WY 28. The concrete bridge is a short distance west of the intersection of the state highway with US 191 in Farson. Two monuments observe the old crossing at a pull-off west of the bridge along the north side of the road. A granite monument makes note of the onetime presence here of a Pony Express station, and a concrete obelisk with an embedded bronze plaque mistakenly states the location as the Little Sandy Crossing where in 1847 Brigham Young met with Jim Bridger. The two did meet at the Little Sandy Crossing, but it wasn't here.

33. Lombard Ferry

From its headwaters in Wyoming's Wind River Range, the Green River flows 730 miles south through southwestern Wyoming into Utah, interrupted only by a small easterly loop into Colorado. At its mouth near Moab, Utah, it serves as one of the largest tributaries of the Colorado River. For pioneers headed toward Fort Bridger, the Green River offered good drinking water, but represented yet another river to cross, and a swift and dangerous one at that.

Depending on the water level and current, emigrants had to choose whether to ford, float, or ferry the Green at its numerous crossing locations. If they chose the latter, the fee generally depended on the same two variables because ferry operators knew they could charge more when river conditions were dangerous. Despite hefty fees, the ferries were quite popular, with emigrants sometimes waiting for days before crossing.

In 1843 a group of mountain men started a ferry operation at one of the Green's most popular crossing locations. The group sold the operation 7 years later to the Mormons, who continued ferry service for another 8 years, during which time it was generally called the Green River Mormon Ferry. The name changed to **Lombard Ferry** following **William Lombard**'s acquisition of the business in the late 1880s.

The Bureau of Land Management manages an attractive visitor site that includes a replica ferry along with interpretive signs beside a walking path alongside the Green River. The site is 22 miles southwest of Farson via WY 28. Heading southwest on WY 28, cross the bridge and take the first left to the site's parking area.

34. Church Butte

Church Butte is an unusual soft sandstone promontory frequently noted in journals by pioneers headed to Fort Bridger. One traveler compared it to a Gothic cathedral, while another likened it to a decorated temple. The butte rises from 75 to 100 feet

Church Butte was frequently noted in the journals of pioneers headed to Fort Bridger.

above the valley floor and is near the old trail whose ruts can still be observed by those willing to park and walk a short distance. As is the case with many remote trail landmarks in Wyoming, at Church Butte you are likely to be by yourself with a landscape that remains largely unchanged since the pioneers passed through.

The landmark is 10 miles southwest of Granger on a gravel road that once served as US 30, a segment of the Lincoln Highway, America's first transcontinental highway. A service station once located across the road from Church Butte during its Lincoln Highway days has since vanished. If approaching from the south on I-80, take exit 53 and head north on Church Butte Road for 5.5 miles. Church Butte will be on the right at the point where the road T's with WY 233.

35. Fort Bridger

Fort Bridger served as an important stop for travelers on the Oregon, California, and Mormon Trails, and later became a hub for railroad employees, Pony Express riders, telegraph workers, and soldiers. The trading post that transitioned into a military post and remained active for nearly 50 years would earn one of the most recognized place names of the American West.

The fort was actually the second trading post of famed mountain man James Bridger, after whom it was named. The first post proved short-lived when Bridger and partner Louis Vasquez established the second post in 1843 to take advantage of the increased number of emigrants heading west. Although the post tended to be viewed poorly by emigrants in comparison to Fort John, which they had visited 380 miles back up the trail, it offered needed supplies, fresh oxen and horses, and a blacksmith shop, all for the right price.

Unlike many early trading posts with life cycles not much longer than pop-up rain showers, Fort Bridger enjoyed a long, if convoluted, life. Bridger's tenure at the post was cut short in 1853 when Brigham Young sent a militia to the fort upon hearing alcohol and ammunition were being sold to American Indians. Bridger learned of the coming of the militia and set sail prior to its arrival. He returned in 1855 and reached an agreement to sell the fort to the Mormons for $8,000, although there is some

Fort Bridger enjoyed an unusually long life as a trading post and, later, a military post. The replica fort is now part of Fort Bridger State Historic Site.

America's Aquarium in Stone

Fossil Butte National Monument, with a treasure lode of fossils, promotes itself as "America's Aquarium in Stone." The unique unit of the National Park Service is a convenient and worthwhile stop for today's travelers exploring the Oregon Trail in southwestern Wyoming.

It is difficult for most of us to imagine this part of the high desert was once a subtropical landscape covered by a huge lake. Millions of years ago the consistency of soil at the bottom of the lake combined with minerals leached from the water proved a perfect formula for preserving organic material on the lake bottom. The result is an abundance of some of the most complete fossils found anywhere in the world. The majority of the fossils are of fish, but fossils of birds, insects, crocodiles, small horses, and plants have also been uncovered here.

The visitor center includes cases of authentic fossils plus a few larger fossil replicas. The latter includes a replica fossil of a 13-foot crocodile, the actual specimen of which is in a museum. Visitors can view a glass-enclosed lab in which a ranger periodically works to uncover a fossil. Two short videos are shown in a small theater room: One addresses the history of the region and the other demonstrates how fossils are discovered and removed from the quarry.

An interesting feature outside the visitor center is a time line along the deck railing that notes events beginning 4.567 billion years ago and continuing to the present. Events noted on plaques along the railing include the extinction of a plant or animal species, along with major geological events such as mountain building.

The monument is in southwestern Wyoming, 12 miles west of Kemmerer via US 30 and CR 300. Phone (307) 877-4455 for information. Kemmerer was home to James Cash Penney's first Golden Rule Store, which grew to become the JC Penney department store chain.

The visitor center at Fossil Butte National Monument offers numerous fossil exhibits.

question if he actually owned the land on which the fort was located. Two years later, following growing animosity between the Mormons and the federal government concerning a variety of issues including polygamy, troops were sent to seize the fort, which the Mormons promptly burned. By 1858 tensions had subsided, and the US Army began construction of a military fort that remained active until 1890.

Today the location of the former fort is part of **Fort Bridger State Historic Site**, which includes numerous historic structures and a replica of the famed trading post. A small museum has exhibits that relate the fort's story from its early years as a trading post through the period it served as an important military post. The historic site, which sits on the old Lincoln Highway, is also home to some wonderfully restored camp cabins that offered overnight rooms to highway travelers in the 1920s and '30s.

From I-80 take exit 34 and drive south for 3 miles to Main Street. The state historic site is on the right.

Guernsey Ruts State Historic Site in southeastern Wyoming is home to deep depressions caused by livestock and pioneer wagons climbing a sandstone hill to avoid marshy soil near the North Platte River.

1. Thomas Fork Crossing
2. Big Hill
3. Peg Leg Smith's Trading Post
4. Soda Springs
5. The Wagon Box Grave
6. Camp Connor
7. Oregon Trail Country Club Swale
8. Sheep Rock
9. Hudspeth's Cutoff
10. Fort Hall
11. American Falls
12. Snake River Overlook
13. Massacre Rocks
14. Register Rock
15. Raft River Crossing
16. Milner Ruts
17. Rock Creek Station and Stricker Homesite
18. Thousand Springs
19. Hagerman Fossil Beds National Monument
20. Three Island Crossing
21. Bonneville Point
22. Oregon Trail Historic Reserve
23. Ward Massacre Site
24. Fort Boise

IDAHO

CRATERS OF
THE MOON

CITY OF ROCKS

IDAHO

Departing Fort Bridger the pioneers entered the southeastern corner of today's Idaho. The emigrant wagon trains soon faced a major climb to a high ridge before descending into the scenic Bear Lake Valley, which proved one of the most pleasant stretches of their long journey. The scenic valley had it all: water, grass, trees, and grand vistas, a combination that offered a welcome change from the arid high desert through which they had been traveling. Bear Lake had been the 1826 and 1827 site for major rendezvous of American Indians, trappers, and traders.

After descending treacherous Big Hill, the emigrants proceeded northwest beside the Bear River past Peg Leg Smith's trading post (1848) toward Fort Hall, an important supply post built in 1834 by a New England businessman who 3 years later sold it to the Hudson's Bay Company. Prior to reaching Fort Hall the emigrants enjoyed a stop at Soda Springs where they sampled one of the trail's natural wonders, carbonated water that some said had the taste of beer. This was also near the location where emigrants heading to California left the main trail.

Until 1852 when Tim Goodale led a large wagon train west along the north side of the Snake toward Boise, the main trail from Fort Hall headed southwest to follow the Snake River's south bank past the rumble of American Falls' 50-foot drop and Register Rock, where many emigrants paused to etch and paint their names on a

William Henry Jackson, *Three Island Crossing* SCBL-(ARCHIVE 43), SCOTTS BLUFF NATIONAL MONUMENT

7-foot-tall basalt boulder. Another several days of travel and they could hear the roar of Shoshone Falls in the distance. A couple of days later they witnessed the strange sight of water gushing from rimrock at Thousand Springs.

Just as the Platte and its two primary tributaries guided pioneers across today's Nebraska and the winding Sweetwater steered emigrants through much of present-day Wyoming, the Snake River served as the emigrants' route across present-day Idaho. Rivers rewarded emigrants with water to drink and grass for their livestock. Well, not always, at least along the Snake. The mighty river certainly moved huge amounts of water, but often through deep canyons that made access to its water nearly impossible.

The Snake River cuts a shallow "U" across southern Idaho before a gradual turn to the northwest and then north to empty its waters into the mighty Columbia. As the river started its curve from the bottom of the "U," wagon trains arrived at Three Island Crossing where many of the pioneers forded to the north bank. Depending on water level and current strength, this was the preferred location to cross and at least temporarily leave the Snake behind by heading north. Those who decided the crossing was too dangerous continued along the south bank, a stretch that was quite difficult.

The main trail followed by pioneers who had crossed the Snake at Three Island Crossing continued northwest to Fort Boise where they had to ford or ferry the river yet again into present-day Oregon. The alternate route south of the river headed northwest and met the main trail a short distance into present-day Oregon. The emigrants still had some distance to travel plus a dangerous and unforgiving river to face, but they were closing in on their destination.

1. Thomas Fork Crossing

Wagon trains entering present-day Idaho encountered **Thomas Fork**, a creek serving as a tributary of the Bear River. Today the stream appears calm, but in the 1840s it made for a difficult crossing due to steep and muddy banks. The issue was resolved for some in the early 1850s when two bridges were constructed, but only for those who could afford the $1-per-wagon fee. Those who could not, or would not, pay the toll either suffered a difficult crossing near the bridges, or traveled a few miles farther and crossed where the land was less marshy.

A pullout on the north side of US 30 approximately 1.5 miles beyond the Wyoming/Idaho border is the site of an interpretive exhibit. The Thomas Fork flows into the Bear River under the bridge a short distance west of the pullout. This is likely near where the wagon trains forded the creek prior to construction of the bridges.

Pioneer wagon trains forded the Thomas Fork close to where the creek empties into the Bear River.

2. Big Hill

Shortly after entering present-day Idaho and crossing Thomas Fork, pioneers were faced with a difficult climb to a high ridge that became known as **Big Hill.** While the climb was strenuous and required double teams of oxen, the more difficult task was a safe descent on the opposite side. The ascent and descent often required most of a day.

Descending Big Hill with covered wagons was dangerous work that required most of the day.

In 1852 an Iowa family stopped for several weeks to construct a road, the McAuley Cutoff, that bypassed the hill and allowed easier access to the Bear Lake Valley. The enterprising family remained at the location for another several weeks to collect tolls from other pioneers who used the cutoff. The path of the old bypass is similar to the route of the current highway.

A large turnout on the east side of US 30, approximately 13 miles north of the Thomas Fork, has interpretive signs about the difficult descent. The hill is about 4 miles south and can be observed from the turnout. A pair of binoculars is helpful but not necessary. The view is impressive, and the path of the old trail as it winds down the hill is evident.

3. Peg Leg Smith's Trading Post

Thomas "Peg Leg" Smith was a colorful character who, beginning in 1848, operated a trading post near the east bank of the Bear River along the Oregon Trail. Smith's primary claim to fame was the self-amputation of his left leg after being shot by an American Indian. Like much of his life history, the source of the injury and resulting amputation depended on who was telling the story. One version from an 1894 issue of the *Los Angeles Herald* claimed Smith was shot by a drunken gambler and his leg amputated by nearby trappers using a butcher knife and handsaw.

Smith was said by some to be a horse thief who claimed to have happened upon a major source of gold but couldn't remember its exact location. An emigrant who stopped at Smith's trading post, a collection of four small log cabins along with several American Indian lodges, wrote in his journal that the owner had "many horses and cattle." Digesting tales of Smith's history, one has to wonder about the source of

Peg Leg Smith, rumored to have amputated his own leg, established a trading post near this site in 1848.

The Bureau of Land Management and America's Historic Trails

Land ownership along the 2,088 miles of the main route of the Oregon Trail is divided about evenly between private and public interests. Within the latter category, the split is about 60 percent federal and 40 percent state. Inclusion of the trail's multiple cutoffs and alternate routes considerably increases the total mileage of paths taken by pioneers to reach Oregon's Willamette Valley. While a substantial portion of the trail has been lost to development and cultivation, hundreds of miles of the original trail remain for today's travelers to enjoy.

No federal agency has been more important in preserving and interpreting the remaining ruts and landmarks of the Oregon Trail than the **Bureau of Land Management (BLM).** The BLM manages 848 miles of the trail, nearly two-thirds of which are in Wyoming. BLM also maintains numerous interpretive sites including Echo Meadows (Oregon), South Pass Overlook (Wyoming), and Milner Historic Recreation Area (Idaho). There are many more. BLM oversees two of the country's most impressive interpretive centers devoted to America's historic trails, one in Casper, Wyoming, and the other in Baker City, Oregon.

The Bureau of Land Management was established in 1946 as a replacement for the General Land Office, an 1816 government creation to support the goal of westward migration and homesteading. BLM administers America's lands—10 percent of the country's land base—that remain from the country's original public domain.

During a 2021 visit to BLM's National Historic Trails Interpretive Center in Casper, we had an opportunity to talk with **Jason Vican,** a BLM visitor information specialist. Our initial question concerned the driving condition of a remote county road that parallels the Oregon Trail west of Casper. Following his assurance we should be okay driving CR 319, the discussion turned to other topics including the connection of BLM with America's historic trails.

On top of Independence Rock, BLM employee Jason Vican (right) assists a visitor locate the name of a relative who was an early pioneer on the Oregon Trail. COURTESY OF BUREAU OF LAND MANAGEMENT

At the time of our meeting, Jason was completing his sixteenth year with the Bureau of Land Management following shorter stints with several state entities including the Wyoming Game and Fish Department and South Dakota's Custer State Park. With regard to the country's historic trails, he commented that nearly everything the interpretive center does—including preparation of its exhibits and galleries, educational programming, youth projects, and off-site trail treks—ties into the pioneer trails. BLM works with a number of partners including the Oregon-California Trails Association and the National Pony Express Association in preserving the trails and educating the public about their history and importance.

Jason views the historic trails as part of a greater story of western expansion. "So many sites are still intact, preserved, and there are numerous journals and diaries which mention these places. People can visit these locations today and make a direct connection to the resources, to the land, and to the story, and feel it, imagine it. These types of influences are meaningful and present unique opportunities in connecting visitors from the present to their past."

According to Jason, the greatest danger to the preservation of the historic trails is future development. One need only view the satellite image of Oregon's Echo Meadows to understand his concern. Excellent trail ruts on a small tract of land under BLM management are surrounded by irrigated cultivation. Without the preservation efforts of the Bureau of Land Management and the organizations with which it cooperates, the living history of America's westward migration would be greatly diminished.

the animals. One certainty is Thomas Smith did operate a trading post, sold whiskey, and sported a peg leg. The accuracy of tales of his other adventures, including friendships with Jim Bridger, Kit Carson, and others, is up for grabs.

The exact site of the old trading post isn't known. An interpretive board placed on the west side of US 30 south of Montpelier by the Idaho Historical Society and Idaho Department of Transportation states the trading post was near the river somewhere in the vicinity of the board.

4. The Magical Waters of Soda Springs

Pioneers following the Bear River north came upon a pleasant diversion from the trail's daily drudgery. They discovered a location that offered sparkling water some claimed tasted like beer. Others chose to add flavoring, such as syrup and sugar, to the carbonated water that surfaced in bubbling pools. What a special experience these travelers took pleasure from in today's Soda Springs, an area that in the 1870s would become a summer home for LDS president Brigham Young.

The delightful springs result from residual geothermal activity in a region with an extensive volcanic

Hooper Springs was the best known of the carbonated cold-water springs in the Soda Springs area.

Pyramid Spring in Soda Springs is now regulated to erupt each hour.

history. During the heating process water combines with carbon dioxide gas, producing the carbonated water the pioneers so enjoyed. The area was rife with these springs during the years pioneers were passing through. Today many of the old springs are gone, some due to climate change, while others became submerged under a 4.5-mile-long man-made reservoir. Despite the reduction in the number of springs, today's visitors are able to enjoy some of the same bubbling waters that enchanted pioneers. Also popular today is an unusual geyser that appeared as a surprise to drillers many years after the era of pioneer travel had ended.

An unpleasant scent of rotten eggs first caught the attention of emigrants passing through the area. Located east of town was the first geothermal landmark for the pioneers. **Sulphur Springs** is a shallow lake or series of small puddles and mud pots, depending on seasonal rainfall. To access the springs, 4 miles east of **Soda Springs** on US 30, turn northeast (right) on Sulphur Canyon Road/Highway 126, drive 1 mile to the first junction, and bear right. The main spring and interpretive exhibits are 50 yards east on Sulphur Canyon Road/Highway 126. The site is on private land.

Hooper Springs, a mile north of town, offered cold, carbonated water. Today the spring is sheltered in a pavilion located in an attractive city park. Entering town on US 30, turn north on 3rd Street and drive about 1.5 miles before turning left on Government Dam Road, which leads to the park.

Coming back into town, turn west (right) on East Hooper Avenue and drive until the avenue T's at Main Street. On the northeast corner is **Octagon Spring Park**. This spring was named for the octagonal canopy placed overhead in the 1890s. Galen Wilson, a local resident, tells us this is his preferred spring for carbonated drinking water.

Cones noted by emigrants at **Pyramid Springs** have mostly been graded away. But a geyser at the same location has become a popular visitor attraction. The geyser, now controlled to erupt each hour, reputedly resulted when drillers hit an artesian well while attempting to locate hot water for mineral baths. The geyser is just down Main Street from Octagon Spring. Drive south on Main Street and the first street to the west (right) will be Geyser Park Street. Interpretive exhibits are at the site.

Steamboat Springs was one of the most frequently mentioned thermal features noted by the pioneers. According to their journals, the spring made a gurgling sound as gas pressure built up sufficiently that warm water was thrust upward with a sound similar to that of a steamboat. In the 1920s the famed spring vanished under 40 feet of water in Alexander Reservoir following the construction of Soda Dam. The spring remains active, and when the reservoir surface is calm, ripples from the thermal activity can be seen.

5. The Wagon Box Grave

A family traveling to Oregon Territory in 1861 fell behind the main wagon train and was attacked by American Indians. All seven members of the family were killed. The family was buried in their own wagon box at the crossing of Little Spring Creek by trappers and other emigrants. The remains were later moved about a half mile northwest to where Fairview Cemetery would later develop.

A pioneer family killed by American Indians after becoming separated from the main wagon train was the first burial at Fairview Cemetery in Soda Springs.

The cemetery is located at the corner of West Center Street and 1st Street West in Soda Springs. From the cemetery entrance the grave is about 200 feet ahead on the right.

6. Camp Connor

Camp Connor was one of numerous small military forts built to offer protection for emigrants traveling along the Oregon Trail. The majority of the army posts, including this one, were short-lived. Camp Connor was established on the north bank of the Bear River in May 1863 and ordered abandoned less than 2 years later in February 1865. **Colonel Connor** is perhaps best known as the US Army officer who led a group of California volunteers to a battle that resulted in the killing of over 250 Shoshone men, women, and children, a conflict that became known as the Bear River Massacre.

Colonel Patrick Edward Connor not only established the military post, one of the earliest in Idaho Territory, with approximately 300 soldiers, but also founded nearby Morristown, a Morrisite settlement of 160 Mormon dissidents he led here from Utah. The settlement proved unsuccessful due in part to early winters resulting in several years of crop failures. Most of the remains of Morristown were flooded by the Alexander Reservoir when the dam was built in 1923.

The former location of Camp Connor can be viewed in the community of Soda Springs by turning south off US 30 onto 3rd Street West. Turn west (right) into the parking lot of the Church of Jesus Christ of Latter-day Saints and drive to the end of the lot facing Alexander Reservoir. Four interpretive exhibits tell the story of the development of Camp Connor and the Soda Springs area.

7. Oregon Trail Country Club Swale

Even travelers who don't know the difference between a driver and a divot will enjoy the magic of a stroll along the most beautiful of depressions from thousands of wagons passing through what is now the **Oregon Trail Country Club.** The swale climbs out of Alexander Reservoir, a body of water created with the 1923 completion of Soda Dam, and parallels the ninth fairway. While today's duffers are swinging away to the northeast toward the ninth hole, the pioneers were moving in the opposite direction toward Fort Hall. Steamboat Springs, a famed geyser noted in many pioneer journals for its peculiar noise, is now submerged in the reservoir, but can be seen on a calm day near the shoreline while walking along the last fairway.

The country club is on the south side of US 30, 2 miles northwest of Soda Springs. Travelers interested in exploring the old trail here should ask permission at the club office. During our third visit to the country club in September 2017, we enjoyed talking with three golfers who had just completed nine holes while snowflakes continued drifting down from the sky.

8. Sheep Rock

Sheep Rock, now called Soda Point, was named by pioneers for the mountain sheep that could sometimes be seen on the high bluff that became a major landmark for early travelers following the Oregon, California, and Mormon Trails. The pioneers had been traveling northwest along the beautiful Bear River Valley when the river took a sharp turn toward the south around Sheep Rock, the northern extremity of

Sheep Rock (now called Soda Point) is the location where pioneers headed to Oregon split from the Bear River, which takes a sharp turn to the south.

the Wasatch Mountain Range. With the river headed to the Great Salt Lake, pioneers with a California destination continued along the Bear River toward the southwest, while those on the main trail to Oregon left the river and moved toward the northwest.

This parting of the ways is perhaps best known as the location where in 1841 the Bidwell-Bartleson Party split with guide Thomas "Broken Hand" Fitzpatrick and headed south, nearly perishing before reaching California. The remaining group members, including Father De Smet, continued along the trail to Oregon.

Sheep Rock is approximately 5 miles west of Soda Springs via US 30. A gravel road to the south off US 30 leads to a parking area with good views of the bluff.

9. Hudspeth's Cutoff

Forty-niners wanted to reach the goldfields of California as quickly as possible following the discovery of gold there in 1848. Emigrants headed to California normally traveled the same trail as pioneers going to Oregon until reaching the Raft River "parting of the ways" in present-day Idaho. **Benoni M. Hudspeth** and **John J. Myers**, two well-traveled mountain men who had previously traveled with John C. Fremont, were leading a company of seventy wagons and about 250 people when in 1849 they blazed a shortcut that would become known as **Hudspeth's Cutoff.**

Hudspeth's Cutoff was used by emigrants heading to California without going to Fort Hall.

The cutoff parted from the Oregon Trail 6 miles west of present-day Soda Springs near Sheep Rock and headed west to rejoin the primary California Trail northeast of City of Rocks. The main trail to Oregon headed northwest from Sheep Rock. The cutoff saved travelers about 25 miles but proved a difficult journey that crossed four mountainous regions and suffered long waterless stretches. While the cutoff failed to save the 49ers much time, it became their preferred route to the California goldfields.

The Idaho Department of Transportation has erected an interpretive sign along US 30 west of Soda Springs to mark the cutoff.

10. Fort Hall

Fort Hall was constructed in 1834 by **Nathaniel Wyeth,** a New England business-man eager to enter what was then a lucrative fur trading business. Wyeth had attended a rendezvous of trappers, traders, and American Indians 2 years earlier and saw the potential of bringing trade goods west and shipping furs back East. After an agreement to supply trade goods to the Rocky Mountain Fur Company went sour, the entrepreneur decided to build his own trading post at a bend in the Snake River in what had proven a prime trapping area.

The fort, consisting of a stockade of cottonwood logs with two blockhouses, was constructed in about 3 weeks. At completion Wyeth headed west where he founded a second trading post, Fort William, near present-day Portland, Oregon.

Unfortunately for the New Englander, the Hudson's Bay Company controlled most of the Northwest's fur trading business and exhibited little interest in dealing with a competitor. In 1834 HBC established its own trading post near the confluence of the Snake and Boise Rivers with a plan to temporarily pay a high price for furs until

Pocatello, Idaho, is home to a replica of Fort Hall, one of the Oregon Trail's oldest and best-known trading posts.

An interior view of the Fort Hall replica.

Wyeth was driven out of business. The plan proved successful and HBC purchased Fort Hall in 1837.

Although the fur business soon entered a period of decline, Hudson's Bay Company decided Fort Hall could remain profitable by servicing emigrants on the Oregon and California Trails. By the mid-1850s a decline in business combined with increasing conflicts with American Indians caused the company to close its Fort Hall operation. Portions of the fort were taken for other uses, and nothing remains of the original trading post. The historic site is now on the Fort Hall Indian Reservation, and access is by reservation only.

The city of Pocatello in 1963 constructed a replica of Fort Hall using plans made available by Hudson's Bay Company. The replica fort is located in Ross Park next to the Bannock County Historical Museum. From I-15 take exit 67 to 5th Avenue, which passes beside the park.

11. American Falls

Pioneers traveling near the south bank of the Snake River were fascinated with the sight and roaring sound of **American Falls.** The falls was reportedly named to differentiate it from Canadian Falls (now Shoshone Falls), 95 miles downstream near today's community of Twin Falls. The cascade was created by an ancient lava flow blockage of the Snake River, resulting in the formation of a lake behind the horseshoe-shaped wall. Rather than a sheer edge, the blockage extended 200 feet, over which the river dropped 50 feet in a series of steps.

A power dam constructed here in 1902 was replaced with a larger irrigation dam in 1927, requiring removal to higher ground of most of the town of American Falls. The remaining structures, including building foundations, are now underwater but sometimes surface during low water levels. In addition to burying the old town, the increased reach of the lake also buried most of the falls and unfortunately covered sections of the old Oregon Trail. A more sturdy replacement for the irrigation dam was built in 1978.

A More Difficult but Safer Route through a Strange Landscape

Wagon trains in the 1860s frequently chose to travel along the 230-mile Goodale Cutoff, which began near Fort Hall, to avoid conflicts with the Shoshone that were occurring on the main trail following the south bank of the Snake River. The cutoff began north of Fort Hall and headed west, skirting the northern edge of today's **Craters of the Moon National Monument and Preserve.** Along parts of the cutoff pioneers traveled through a strange land of ancient lava flows that originated from fissures in the earth. Choosing the cutoff proved to be a grueling two- to three-week trip.

The national monument is home to sixty lava flows and twenty-five cones in one of America's most unusual landscapes. Evidence of past volcanic activity includes lava flows, spatter cones, cinder cones, and even lava tube caves. The molten rock rose to the surface through a series of fissures in the earth's crust called the Great Rift. Cinder cones line this rift.

The lava was created during eight different eruptions stretching from 2,000 to 15,000 years ago. The time between eruptive periods averaged 2,000 years. The last eruption occurred over 2,000 years ago, but don't let this dissuade you from a visit.

The monument's visitor center offers exhibits that include pioneer travel through the park's edge. An excellent film explains the geology and creation of this unusual part of Idaho. Hiking trails and a 7-mile scenic drive provide access to many of the park's features. Markers along US 20 identify the approximate route of pioneers choosing to travel the Goodale Cutoff.

Craters of the Moon National Monument and Preserve is administered by the National Park Service and located in the Snake River Plain of central Idaho. The park lies between the towns of Arco and Carey on US 20.

Pioneer wagon trains found it rough going along the Goodale Cutoff.

American Falls was noted in numerous pioneer journals.

To access American Falls, take exit 40 off I-86. Turn right onto ID 39 but keep left at the fork where ID 39 turns right. This road, Pocatello Avenue, parallels I-86. Follow it to Bannock Avenue and turn left. Follow Bannock until it T's into Taylor Street and turn right. Take the first left at Falls Avenue and follow the road to its end at the Snake River where there is a parking area, a viewpoint of the remaining falls, and a 1915 Meeker-inspired monument. For river access return one block on Falls Avenue and turn right onto Valdez Street, which leads to the Oregon Trail River Access, where docks and a path along the Snake River are located.

12. Snake River Overlook

For most travelers on I-86, the rest stop west of American Falls warrants a short stop if only to enjoy the outstanding view of the **Snake River.** For those interested in the Oregon Trail, the stop serves as the beginning location for a 0.5-mile trail that leads to impressive trail ruts on the opposite side of the interstate.

The trail begins at a kiosk with interpretive exhibits located in a grassy area on the west end of the rest stop's one-way loop drive. Drive past the restrooms and along the loop drive to the kiosk and park. The paved trail leads downhill and through tunnels under both lanes of I-86. Ruts of the Oregon Trail are visible shortly after the walking path emerges from the second tunnel.

The Snake River Overlook offers an outstanding river view along with access to Oregon Trail ruts.

The rest stop is 5 miles west of American Falls at milepost 31 and is accessible only from the interstate's westbound lane. Those traveling eastbound can move to the westbound lane 5 miles east at the exit to Rock Creek Road.

13. Massacre Rocks

Pioneers following the south bank of the Snake River from American Falls were concerned about the possibility of attack by American Indians as they approached the narrow passage through what became known as "Massacre Rocks." Initially called "Devil's Gate," the area of large boulders along the river was renamed "Massacre Rocks" following a series of conflicts between the Shoshone and emigrant wagon trains east of Devil's Gate during August 1862. Emigrant concern was sufficiently great that many wagon trains chose to travel the Goodale Cutoff through today's Craters of the Moon National Monument in order to avoid potential issues with tribes along the Snake River route.

The giant rocks in what is now **Massacre Rocks State Park** are remnants of an extinct volcano. Boulders ended up in their present location as a result of massive floodwaters that barreled down the Snake River Valley over 14,000 years ago. Many of the giant rocks were removed during construction of the interstate. While the pioneers were most likely unappreciative of the rugged beauty of an area in which they worried about being attacked, today's travelers can camp, hike, picnic, rock climb, play disc golf, or rent a cabin in the state park. Oregon Trail ruts are visible on the south side of the interstate with access at nearby Snake River Overlook. A park

Pioneers were concerned the large boulders could be hiding Indigenous people preparing to attack.

visitor center contains fossil displays, interpretive exhibits of Oregon Trail history, and a small gift shop.

The state park is located 15 miles southwest of American Falls. From I-86 use either exit 36 or exit 21 to access the park.

14. Register Rock

The pioneers had traveled over 1,200 miles by the time they reached a popular overnight spot beside Rock Creek, which empties into the nearby Snake River. While dinner was being cooked and preparations made for the following day's journey, some emigrants took time to search for a surface on which they could etch or paint their name with axle grease.

Fortunately for today's travelers and history buffs, a thoughtful Idahoan made the decision to spend some state money on covering and fencing a large, round basalt boulder that served as a tablet for many pioneers. A number of names that were incised remain legible over a century and a half later in what has become known as **Register Rock.**

Emigrant signatures on Register Rock.

Of particular interest are two images chipped out of a nearby rock in 1866 by 6-year-old J. J. Hansen. One is of an American Indian chief. Hansen, who not surprisingly grew up to become a sculptor, returned to the area in 1908 and etched the new date on his artwork.

Register Rock served as a register for pioneers who wished to etch their names in the large boulder.

The state historic site is 12 miles southwest of American Falls in Massacre Rocks State Park. From I-86 take exit 28 and turn south on Register Road to cross the interstate bridge, then follow the road 2 miles to Register Rock. The rock is in a quiet area perfect for a picnic lunch.

15. Raft River Crossing

Emigrants following the south bank of the Snake River had an important decision to make about a dozen miles following their departure from Register Rock. At a fork in the trail, they could choose the left branch to the southwest and City of Rocks before traveling through Nevada to California. Alternatively, they could continue along the south side of the Snake River toward Oregon Territory. By one estimate a third of the 49ers used this cutoff on their way to the California goldfields.

The actual fork in the trail, sometimes called "parting of the ways," is on private property and inaccessible to today's travelers. A monument with an interpretive plaque is near a farmhouse and large parking area. From I-86 take exit 15 and turn south on Yale Road for about 1.7 miles. The monument is on the left in front of a white fence.

16. Milner Ruts

Several miles of excellent trail ruts resulting from thousands of pioneer wagons traveling along the south side of the Snake River are easily accessible in **Milner Historic Recreation Area.** The recreation area is managed by the Bureau of Land

Milner Historic Recreation Area, west of Burley, preserves some excellent trail ruts for travelers to explore.

The main route of the California Trail passed through City of Rocks.

City of Rocks National Reserve: A Most Unusual Place

City of Rocks National Reserve in southern Idaho is one of only two national reserves managed by the National Park Service. The reserve, shaped by volcanic eruptions of widely differing time periods, offers visitors an unusual landscape in which granite rocks appear to be growing out of the ground. The oldest and darker rocks were formed 2.5 billion years ago and the youngest, lighter rocks are about 30 million years old. The odd appearance of the rocks stems from millions of years of erosion.

Thousands of years before the arrival of emigrants, the area around City of Rocks was occupied by ancestors of the Shoshone and Paiute. This land served as their hunting grounds and was the source of pine nuts picked from the pinyon pine forests.

City of Rocks National Reserve includes a section of the California Trail that was also used by pioneers following the Applegate Trail to Oregon. The cutoff departed the main route near Twin Falls and dipped south into Nevada to follow the Humboldt River and approach present-day Oregon from the south. Debuting in 1846, the cutoff was promoted as safer than the main route along the Snake River.

When wagon trains started rolling through the area in 1843, emigrants were fascinated by the masses of rock formations. National reserve researchers have collected entries from emigrant journals. In one 1850 entry, Lucena Parsons predicted, "A few more years & they will be leveled with the ground. They look at a distance like a ruined city." Probably the most quoted journal entry was written in 1849 by James Wilkins: "We encamped at the city of the rocks, a noted place from the granite rocks rising abruptly out of the ground. They are in a romantic valley clustered together, which gives them the appearance of a city."

When the emigrants stopped at noon or settled in for the evening, many used axle grease to write their names on the large rocks. Along the reserve's California Trail Corridor, twenty-two rocks with emigrant signatures remain visible for today's visitors. Research by reserve employees has resulted in short histories, some with pictures, of many individuals whose names appear on the rocks.

Today, City of Rocks is mostly used for recreation. In addition to enjoying the amazing rock formations, visitors come to fish, hike, mountain bike, and horseback ride. The reserve is especially well known by rock climbers, who have over 1,000 traditional and bolt-protected routes to climb.

The reserve is located at the southern end of the Albion Mountains in south-central Idaho, a few miles from the Utah border. It is about an hour's drive south from the main route of the Oregon Trail near Twin Falls.

Management and includes campsites, interpretive exhibits, picnic sites, and boat ramps along 4 miles of Snake River shoreline.

A 1.3-mile paved walking trail parallels the historic trail ruts through the middle of the recreation area. An information kiosk is at the west terminus of the walking trail. This is a worthwhile stop for travelers interested in experiencing a relative lengthy walk along some pristine trail ruts.

From the town of Burley drive 4 miles west on US 30. As the road begins a turn toward the south, turn right onto 500 West and then immediately left onto West Milner Road. Follow West Milner Road approximately 2 miles, a stretch that includes a 90-degree curve to the south. Take the first right after the curve and continue on West Milner Road for a little less than 3 miles; the west entrance to the recreation area will be on the right. It is likely you will be alone on the walking path following the old trail.

17. Rock Creek Station and Stricker Homesite

At a point where the Oregon Trail converged with two stage routes, **Rock Creek** became a popular stopover for trail traffic moving along the south bank of the Snake River. Emigrants typically arrived during the heat of August, so a source of fresh water resulted in the area becoming a popular campground. The later addition of a trading post offered another reason for emigrants to spend some time here.

Initial development at Rock Creek consisted of a home station for a mail service between Salt Lake City and Walla Walla in Washington Territory. In short order the lone trading post between Fort Hall and Fort Boise opened in 1865. The store was sold in 1876 to **Herman Stricker,** who homesteaded here and continued the store's operation until 1897.

Rock Creek Station was a popular stop for pioneers traveling along the south side of the Snake River.

The **Stricker Store**, a pioneer cemetery, the **Stricker home**, and various outbuildings are at the site. A new interpretive center offers exhibits along with eleven informative signs that provide a history of the site. A stone wet cellar once used to store liquor and other bottled goods was next to a saloon that is no longer standing. A nearby dry cellar was used for storage of goods such as flour and sugar.

An interpretive plaque at Rock Creek Station.

The Stricker home, built in 1900 following the loss of their original log home by fire, is open for guided tours on Sundays.

From Twin Falls head east on US 30 and continue through Kimberly until the highway jogs to the southeast. Leave US 30 and continue straight south on CR 3500 East. At a golf driving range turn east on East 3200 North (Pumpland Road) and drive about 2 miles. The home and store are on the south side of the road. The buildings are open Sunday afternoons. Self-guided tours are available daily. Phone (208) 423-4000 for information.

18. Thousand Springs

Pioneers traveling along the south side of the Snake River on their way to a popular river crossing location came across a memorable sight—water gushing below the rimrock along a canyon wall lining the opposite bank. The water wasn't spurting from one or two or even a dozen places, but all along the wall to create numerous waterfalls that cascaded into the river.

The multiple springs result from the Snake River taking a northern turn and cutting into a large aquifer augmented by sources of water as far away as the Lost River, which disappears into a sink

Pioneers passing by Thousand Springs were fascinated with water gushing from rimrock above the Snake River.

nearly 100 miles north. Water can flow underground for long distances through the porous volcanic rock that underlies this region.

The springs have been in decline for the last several decades due to changes in climate along with increased pumping of groundwater for irrigation. Still, **Thousand Springs** remains an impressive sight for today's travelers, as it was for the pioneers. The springs are now part of Idaho's Thousand Springs State Park, which encompasses six units. The springs can be viewed from US 30 (1000 Springs Scenic Byway). A pullout on the south side of the road has signs with information about Thousand Springs.

19. Hagerman Fossil Beds National Monument

Emigrants continuing along the south bank of the Snake River arrived, usually in the heat of July, at the southern end of today's **Hagerman Fossil Beds National Monument.** By now they had walked nearly 1,300 miles. Here the bank ascends sharply, forming 600-foot-high bluffs. Wagon trains frequently stopped for the night near the base of the cliffs where water was easily accessible. American Indians in the area, the Shoshone-Bannock and Shoshone-Paiute tribes, often greeted the wagon trains to trade dried fish including salmon, sturgeon, and steelhead trout.

The following day's travel included a steep, difficult, hot, and dusty climb to reach a plateau at the top of the bluffs. Some of the pioneers might have found a fossil or two as they climbed the bank, since it was these treasures that persuaded the federal government to set aside the area as a national monument.

The monument's entry road follows the historic trail from US 30, and rut segments are visible while traveling the road. An overlook at mile 10.3 along the entry road has a parking area and a 0.5-mile loop trail with interpretive exhibits and excellent views of the Snake River Plain. The location allows visitors to gain a close-up view of the trail ruts.

Hagerman Fossil Beds National Monument contains excellent trail ruts and offers outstanding views of the Snake River Valley.

Fossils have been found in various layers of the bluffs. The fossil record here spans 550,000 years, from discoveries 3.7 million years old at river level to 3.15 million years old at the top of the bluffs. Over 200 species of animal and plant fossils have been discovered including 8 species found nowhere else.

The first to excavate the bluffs were paleontologists from the Smithsonian Institution in 1929 after a local rancher came across the fossil beds. The most famous fossil discovered is known as the Hagerman Horse, a zebralike ancestor of today's horse. Twenty complete skeletons and 120 horse skulls have been found. Also discovered in the bluffs were fossils of mastodons, saber-toothed cats, camels, and ground sloths.

The visitor center for Hagerman Fossil Beds National Monument is about 6 miles northeast of Hagerman at 2314 S. Ritchie Road in Thousand Springs State Park. Phone (208) 933-4105 for information.

20. Three Island Crossing

The Snake River cut a deep path through present-day Idaho. Swift currents and high canyon walls made it difficult for the pioneers to access water from the river, let alone cross to the north bank where better vegetation and smoother travel awaited. While danger accompanied any crossing attempt, a wide bay-like section of the river populated with three islands became a popular place for many wagon trains to ford.

The **Three Island Crossing** offered pioneers stepping-stones to assist their crossing to the north bank. Wagons crossed a relatively shallow section of the river onto the southern-most of the three islands before encountering the most dangerous section—the river's main channel. The third and northernmost island was generally bypassed during the crossings. Depending on current strength, men on each side of

Depending on the water level and current, emigrant wagon trains often forded to the north bank of the Snake River at Three Island Crossing.

The descent to the south bank of the Snake River at Three Island Crossing can easily be seen from near the park's visitor center.

the river might use ropes attached to the wagons to assist with the crossing. In addition, two and three wagons might be lashed side by side to provide greater weight that offered resistance to the current.

Not all emigrants decided to cross at this location. On occasions when the river flow was too strong, pioneers continued along the south bank, which entailed a rough and arid trip that didn't merge with the main trail until north of the current Idaho-Oregon border.

The crossing is now part of a wonderful state park that opened in 1971. The park offers two campgrounds, a day-use area, and an interesting interpretive center devoted to the historic trail. Visitors can walk from the interpretive center along a path that leads to the north bank of the Snake where pioneer wagons emerged from the river. The trail's approach to the south bank is clearly visible from the north side of the river. The park also includes a section of land along the south bank with an outstanding view of the three islands. If you are heading north, ask at the interpretive center about the Oregon Trail Backcountry Byway, which connects Three Island Crossing with Bonneville Point.

The park is accessed from I-84 by taking Glenn's Ferry exit 121 (westbound) or exit 120 (eastbound) into town to Commercial Street, which changes to West Madison and leads to the park entrance. We enjoyed the park so much during our 2010 visit we decided to stay an additional night. Phone (208) 366-2394 for park information.

21. Bonneville Point

When **Benjamin Bonneville**'s expedition reached the summit of a promontory over-looking a scenic valley in 1833, he reportedly said, *"Les bois; les bois; voyez le bois,"* translated as "The woods; the woods; see the woods." The valley and city now bear the name Boise, and the summit was later named Bonneville Point. At the time the French-born explorer and West Point graduate was on leave from the US Army on what would become a three-year exploratory trip through much of the Northwest. Reaching the summit of what is now **Bonneville Point,** the captain was following an old American Indian trail that within a decade would become the main road for pioneers headed to Oregon.

Bonneville was an impressive individual who was trusted by the American Indians and may well have enjoyed a successful career in commerce had he not come up against the Hudson's Bay Company, which had already locked up business with many tribes. As it was, Bonneville returned to Missouri where he resumed a military career that included participation in the Mexican-American War and the Civil War. He died in 1878 at age 82 in Fort Smith, Arkansas.

The site includes a pavilion with information panels, but the main attraction is the panoramic view of the Boise River Valley and the wagon ruts that intercept the site and descend the hill toward the Boise River. To access Bonneville Point take exit 64 off I-84 and drive east 2.5 miles to the site's access road.

Trail ruts descend from Bonneville Point toward the Boise River. Interpretive signs are in a pavilion overlooking the valley.

22. Oregon Trail Historic Reserve

Oregon Trail Historic Reserve is a 77-acre Boise city park with undisturbed wagon ruts through the middle of the long, narrow reserve. The trail includes the Kelton Ramp, cut from basalt rimrock in the 1860s to connect the second and third terraces above the Boise River.

The reserve, located in a residential area on the southeast edge of Boise, offers gravel walking trails that circle the reserve and connect to different areas of the neighborhood. A small parking area with restroom facilities is available. The reserve is a joint venture of the city of Boise, the Bureau of Land Management, and residents of Surprise Valley.

The reserve is at 4500 E. Lake Forest Drive. Turn left off ID 21 onto East Lake Forest Drive, which curves toward the right to the parking area. Directly across ID 21 is the entrance to Oregon Trail Recreation Area and Trailhead–Ada County Park, which also contains trail ruts. This park includes a display area at the east end of the parking lot. On this side of ID 21 the trail comes in from the southeast and remains on the west side of the power lines. Here you are encouraged to walk in the trail ruts.

The Kelton Ramp was used by emigrants to access the Snake River. The ramp is part of Boise's Oregon Trail Historic Reserve.

OCTA: Guardian of the Historic Trails

Oregon-California Trails Association president James Briggs enjoys a working vacation on the Lander Road.

Historic trails and their associated landmarks are fragile pieces of America's national heritage. They are subject to a continuous battle with nature pummeling them with rain, ice, and wind that gradually erase emigrant names inscribed or painted on stone and erodes ruts left by thousands of pioneer wagons in the mid-nineteenth century. The trails and landmarks are also subject to destruction by humans through development and vandalism. Cultivation and construction have destroyed hundreds of miles of historic trails. Once lost, these remnants of American history are forever gone. Fortunately, men and women with a common interest in our country's past have joined together to preserve the legacy of America's historic trails.

The **Oregon-California Trails Association (OCTA)** was organized in the early 1980s to protect the historic emigrant trails. Headquartered near the National Frontier Trails Museum in Independence, Missouri, the organization and its 1,600 members work not only to preserve remnants of the historic trails, but to encourage research and educate the public about one of the most inspiring periods in America's history.

The parent organization is supported by eleven regional chapters, mostly in the West and Northwest where a large portion of the country's historic trails are located. Regional chapters primarily work on local issues such as seeking land easements for trail segments, researching laws that can be useful in mitigating damage from planned development, and mapping and marking trails.

John Briggs, OCTA's president at the time this book was published, was born and raised in England. This seemed somewhat surprising until we learned his employment as an engineer involved locations all over the world. It should also be noted he had the good sense to marry an American gal and currently resides in Boise, Idaho, within walking distance of some excellent Oregon Trail ruts.

John's passion for history was launched in the 1990s when he and his wife, Nancy, transferred back to England where they lived in a historic home and attended a nearby fourteenth-century church. Following their return to the United States, the couple moved into an area of southeast Boise that is home to the Oregon Trail Historic Reserve, the 77-acre city park that preserves remnants of the trail.

The OCTA president said a major amount of members' efforts are directed toward protecting the trails from damage associated with wind farms, electric transmission lines, pipelines, road construction, housing and mining developments, and vandalism. To be effective at these tasks requires that the organization have precise mapping and marking of the trails along with research to support their work. In 2020 the organization's members logged over 330,000 volunteer hours at these types of activities.

Readers with an interest in supporting this worthwhile organization's work should consider becoming a member of OCTA. For information visit www.octa-trails.org and click on the upper left tab, "Discover OCTA."

23. Ward Massacre Site

In August 1854 five wagons with twenty people, including the **Alexander Ward** family, were headed to Fort Boise when they got separated from the main wagon train. The group had stopped near present-day Caldwell, Idaho, when a band of Shoshone approached and asked to purchase some horses. When the request was denied, the American Indians departed but later returned to steal a horse. This was followed by a return of more American Indians who mutilated the entire group with the exception of two of the Ward boys who managed to hide in the bushes after being wounded with arrows.

US Army troops subsequently pursued the Shoshone with a retribution so severe the local tribes became incensed, resulting in ensuing battles that caused the abandonment of both Fort Boise and Fort Hall. Emigrant wagon trains had almost no protection along that part of the Oregon Trail until 1863. In January of that year, the US Army killed over 250 Shoshone men, women, and children in what became known as the Bear River Massacre. This ended Shoshone attacks on the emigrants who were crossing and, in some cases, settling on Shoshone land in the Northwest.

The Ward Massacre site is at **Ward Memorial Park** in Caldwell, Idaho. The park includes a tall granite monument with an attached bronze plaque with the names and ages of members of the wagon train. An interpretive information board is nearby. Follow US 26 west out of Boise approximately 19 miles to Middleton Road. Turn north (right) and drive 1 mile to Lincoln Road. Turn east (right), and the small county park is on the north side of the road.

24. Fort Boise

Fort Boise (often called "Old" Fort Boise following the 1863 construction of a military post of the same name in today's capital city of Boise) was built in 1834 by Thomas McKay of the Hudson's Bay Company. At the time HBC wanted to compete with Fort Hall, a new trading post that had been built 300 miles east earlier the same year by Nathaniel Wyeth's American Fur Company. Wyeth sold Fort Hall in 1837 to Hudson's Bay Company, which made it the firm's primary regional trading post.

Fort Boise was rebuilt in 1838 near the confluence of the Boise and Snake Rivers. Although the fur trade had experienced a serious decline, the fort became a popular stop for emigrants traveling the Oregon Trail. By this time the fort's stockade of poles had been covered with adobe and blockhouses added to offer protection from American Indian attack. Many of the emigrants forded or ferried the Snake River near the fort.

A replica of Old Fort Boise trading post is located in Parma. The original fort is long gone.

A major flood seriously damaged the fort in 1853, and Fort Boise was abandoned the following year after a war party of the Shoshone and the Snake decimated a wagon train headed to the fort. Today the fort's location is thought to be underwater.

An unusual cement monument with a lion's head allegedly represents the approximate location of the old fort. To reach the monument, drive north on US 95 through Parma until reaching Old Fort Boise Road and turn left (west). Drive to the end of the road that enters Fort Boise Wildlife Management Area. Bear left and follow the gravel road to the river. Turn right at the river and drive to the large parking area with a bathroom. Park and walk along a trail that begins at the north end of the parking lot. The monument is on the left beside the river. We found it quite difficult to locate the monument as it was surrounded by thick vegetation. A replica of Old Fort Boise is in the nearby town of Parma at 109 Parma Road.

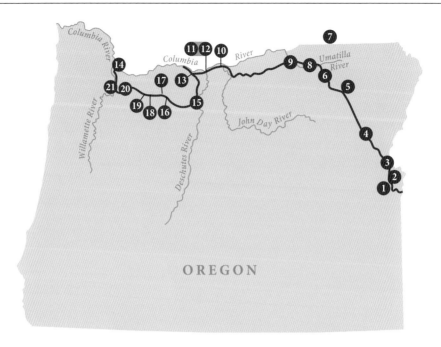

1 Keeney Pass
2 John D. Henderson Grave
3 Farewell Bend
4 Flagsaff Hill
5 Birnie Park
6 Blue Mountain Crossing
7 Whitman Mission (Washington)
8 Lower Umatilla River Crossing
9 Echo Meadows
10 John Day River Crossing
11 Descent to the Columbia River
12 Deschutes River Crossing
13 Fort Dalles
14 Fort Vancouver (Washington)
15 Tygh Valley
16 Barlow Pass
17 Pioneer Woman's Grave
18 Laurel Hill Chute
19 Barlow Road Tollgate
20 Philip Foster Farm
21 John McLoughlin Home in Oregon City

OREGON

Following a stop to rest and acquire supplies at Fort Boise, pioneers either forded or ferried across the Snake River into present-day Oregon, where they headed northwest to meet the mighty Columbia River. Six miles after crossing, the wagon trains were joined by emigrants who had chosen to continue along the south side of the Snake rather than ford at Three Island Crossing. From this joining of the trails, the combined wagon trains climbed relatively gentle Keeney Pass, where excellent ruts remain visible to today's travelers.

Crossing the Malheur River where there were hot springs along the banks for bathing, the pioneers veered north toward Farewell Bend where they would bid goodbye to the Snake, a largely inaccessible river they had been following for over 300 miles. Then it was northwest through Virtue Flat, passing along the southwest shoulder of Flagstaff Hill across Baker Valley to the bowl-shaped Grande Ronde. Here the trail turned west toward the scenic Blue Mountains, which offered a welcome change from the rugged and mostly lifeless terrain over which the pioneers had been traveling.

During the early 1840s pioneers crossed the Umatilla River and headed north for a stop at Whitman Mission. Some then chose to raft down the Columbia while others followed the river's south side to reach The Dalles. Traffic to the mission tapered off

William Henry Jackson, *Blue Mountains* SCBL-(ARCHIVE 44), SCOTTS BLUFF NATIONAL MONUMENT

after 1844 and dried up following the 1847 killing of Marcus Whitman and his wife, Narcissa, by Cayuse.

Pioneers who chose to avoid the loop to Whitman Mission headed west after crossing 3,622-foot Deadman Pass and leaving the Blue Mountains. The trail crossed to the north side of the Umatilla River in present-day Pendleton and followed the Umatilla west for 25 miles, crossing the river once again at present-day Echo. The highlands across this part of today's Oregon presented some of the harshest country the pioneers encountered during the entire trip, and it would continue to The Dalles where the early trail ended.

The main trail continued west from the Umatilla, crossing Willow Creek before arriving at McDonald Ford on the John Day River. It then continued mostly west until nearing the Columbia on a high bluff where pioneers caught their initial view of the mighty river. The wagons descended to the bottomland to ford the Deschutes River near its mouth, and then ascended a hill and continued overland to The Dalles. Prior to the 1845 arrival of Sam Barlow, The Dalles was the end of the Oregon Trail. From this point emigrants either disposed of their wagons and most of their remaining personal items to continue on foot along the south bank of the Columbia or paid to raft the wagons down the Columbia to Fort Vancouver and then ferry across the Columbia to the Willamette River.

Kentuckian Sam Barlow and his extended family arrived at The Dalles in 1845 where they found a long wait and high prices. Barlow decided to see if he could find an overland route to the Willamette Valley by rounding the south shoulder of Mount Hood. The overland route through a dense forest opened the following year as a toll road. The emigrants now had the option of avoiding the cost and danger of rafting down the Columbia. Barlow's road terminated at Oregon City, which in 1848 became the Oregon Territory's first capital.

1. Keeney Pass

After fording the Snake River near Fort Boise, the pioneers headed northwest to meet the Columbia River. The day's hot and dusty journey would generally end at the Malheur River where they would spend the night after bathing in the hot springs. Along the way the wagons had merged to climb the relatively gentle hill leading to **Keeney Pass.** During the approach and climb toward the pass, emigrant wagon trains left ruts that can be explored by today's travelers along a parallel gravel hiking path.

The Bureau of Land Management has preserved a segment of excellent wagon ruts that are accessible at the Keeney Pass Interpretive Site. The site is named for a young trapper and guide, **Jonathan Keeney,** who joined Jim Bridger and later established a ferry near Fort Boise.

A view to the north near the beginning of the climb toward Keeney Pass.

The BLM site has interpretive panels and provides a path that follows the ruts as they ascend to Keeney Pass. The interpretive site is 6 miles southeast of Vale on Lytle Boulevard, a paved county road.

2. John D. Henderson Grave

After an aborted start in 1852, the following year the family of John and Mary Ann Henderson departed their Missouri home as part of a major wagon train headed for Oregon. After crossing into today's Oregon, **John Henderson** died a short distance south of the Malheur River on August 9, 1853. The cause of death isn't clear, although the monument states: "Died of Thirst, August 9, 1852, Unaware of Nearness of Malheur River." The family continued on to the Willamette Valley, and Mary Henderson remarried the following year.

The grave is on private property 0.8 mile south of Vale near a gravel parking area off Lytle Boulevard. Park and walk north around a closed gate to view the monument. An interpretive panel placed by the Oregon-California Trails Association is on the right just south of the gate.

3. Farewell Bend

The Oregon Trail closely tracked the Snake River from Fort Hall to Old Fort Boise on today's Idaho/Oregon border. Shortly before the Snake reaches the border, it curves northwest and then northeast. This is where the wagon trains pulled away from the mighty river they had followed for 300 miles. The pioneers generally spent one last night camped beside the river before bidding it a final farewell and continuing their journey to the northwest.

The area where the pioneers camped is now part of **Farewell Bend State Recreation Area.** The park has interpretive displays about the Oregon Trail and earlier mountain men including Captain Benjamin Bonneville in 1833 and John C. Fremont and his party in 1843, who spent time in the area. The park includes a campground and offers a variety of recreational activities.

No trail ruts remain in the recreation area, but some excellent swales are nearby on BLM land. To explore the swales, take I-84 exit 353 and turn left to drive under the interstate to Lockett Road. Follow Lockett Road while watching for a fork with Lockett Road heading to the right. Continue following Lockett to the Birch Creek Trail Site, less than a mile from the fork.

At Farewell Bend the pioneers bid good-bye to the Snake River they had been following for 300 miles.

The Birch Creek Trail Site near Farewell Bend Recreation Area offers excellent swales of the old trail.

To visit Farewell Bend State Recreation Area, take exit 353 on I-84 and follow US 30. The address is 23751 Old Hwy. 30, Huntington.

4. Flagstaff Hill

Flagstaff Hill is best known by today's travelers as the home of the National Historic Oregon Trail Interpretive Center, an impressive facility operated by the Bureau of Land Management. For pioneers of the 1800s the hill was just another oversized mound to circumvent on the way to the Willamette Valley. Emigrant wagon trains approached Flagstaff Hill from the southeast along Virtue Flat before rounding the hill on the south and heading northwest through 20-mile-long Baker Valley.

Having traveled 1,600 miles from their start in Independence, Missouri, most pioneers had little interest in climbing 400-plus feet to the top of Flagstaff Hill. Had they done so they would have enjoyed a panoramic view of the valley that would lead them to their next obstacle, the Blue Mountains, which could be seen in the distance. Today's travelers are able to drive to the top of the hill and tour one of the country's premier interpretive centers. A walking trail from the interpretive center winds down the hill to reach the path of the Oregon Trail.

Flagstaff Hill is located 5 miles east of Baker City, on OR 86. From I-86 take exit 302 and head east.

Looking northwest from the top of Flagstaff Hill provides a view of the Blue Mountains.

The wagons are circled atop Flagstaff Hill at the National Historic Oregon Trail Interpretive Center.

Historic Baker City

Present-day **Baker City** is in a picturesque and rugged area of eastern Oregon that in the 1840s served as a popular overnight camping spot for emigrants traveling the Oregon Trail. Following the 1861 discovery of gold, it became much more than an overnight stop. Today the town is a popular destination for travelers who wish to explore one of the country's outstanding interpretive centers devoted to the Oregon Trail.

Baker City was incorporated in 1874 and named for **Edward Dickinson Baker,** Oregon's first senator and the only active member of Congress killed during the Civil War. Mining, ranching, and the timber industry supported the town in its early years. Things picked up in 1884 with the arrival of the Oregon Railway & Navigation Company and the Oregon Short Line Railroad, which opened up an opportunity for commerce with distant markets.

With a population of 6,700 in 1900, Baker City was the largest community between Portland and Salt Lake City. It was home to saloons, gambling houses, and dance halls, but also boasted fine hotels, restaurants, and the Baker Theater opera house.

After an 1887 fire destroyed many of the town's buildings, new homes and commercial buildings were constructed of brick and masonry rather than wood. Tuff, a porous rock with a distinctive texture formed from volcanic ash and quarried from south of town, was used in constructing several buildings including City Hall, the Carnegie Library, and St. Francis Cathedral.

Baker City's first elegant hotel, the Warshauer, was constructed in 1889 with a tuff foundation. The hotel offered seventy guest rooms, a dining room with seating for 200, and many special features for its era, including private baths and an elevator. Its most distinctive feature was a large cupola with a clock on the building's corner. In 1895 the hotel was purchased by a group of investors who changed the name to Geiser Grand Hotel. The hotel closed in 1968, but was reopened under new ownership in 1998 following a $7 million restoration.

Today Baker City is a hub for tourism with recreational opportunities including the outstanding National Historic Oregon Trail Interpretive Center. If time allows, spend a night or two in downtown's Geiser Grand and enjoy a walking tour of the historic district.

5. Birnie Park

The city of La Grande rests in the Grande Ronde Valley surrounded by the scenic Blue Mountains. Pioneer wagon trains had a grueling descent into the valley and a strenuous climb out due to the steep valley walls. The valley itself was a bit of a haven for the emigrants, who frequently stopped for the night in the area where **George S. Birnie Park** is now located. The following morning the grounds served as a staging area where oxen teams would be combined in order to be able to pull the wagons up the 1,000-foot climb out of the valley

Birnie Park is at the corner of B Avenue (the Oregon Trail) and Gekeler Lane. The pleasant neighborhood park offers picnic tables and a children's playground that includes a wrought-iron outline of a covered wagon. A sidewalk is lined with Oregon

The area that is now part of La Grande's Birnie Park once served as a camping and staging area for pioneers headed out of the Grande Ronde Valley.

Trail–related interpretive exhibits and eight glazed ceramic columns with abstract designs symbolizing the emigrants' journey through the valley.

To follow the Oregon Trail through town, continue down B Avenue to a "Meeker Marker" that sits in the front yard of a home at the southwest corner of B Avenue and Walnut Street. Although the trail continues up the hill, B Avenue comes to a dead end.

6. Blue Mountain Crossing

The emigrants had navigated the Rocky Mountains by crossing the gentle grade leading to South Pass in southwestern Wyoming. The Blue Mountains of eastern Oregon and Washington were not quite so welcoming. Heading northwest out of the Grande Ronde Valley, emigrant wagon trains were required to climb nearly 1,000 feet toward Deadman Pass. On the plus side, the ponderosa pine and Douglas fir enveloping "the Blues" were a welcome change from hundreds of miles of rough and arid landscape that surrounded much of the Snake River.

The Oregon Trail Interpretive Park at **Blue Mountain Crossing** is an excellent place to view the trail and imagine pioneer wagons crossing the Blue Mountains. Administered by the US Forest Service, the interpretive park includes a 0.5-mile footpath with display panels beside two wide trail depressions, one resulting from freight wagons and another carved by emigrant wagons rolling through a heavily forested ridge of the Blue Mountains.

To access the interpretive park, drive 10.5 miles west of La Grande on I-84, taking exit 248 onto Spring Creek Road. Drive 0.2 mile and turn right on Old Emigrant Hill Scenic Frontage Road. Drive 0.7 mile and take the first road (Farm Road 1843) to the right and drive 2.4 miles to the park. The interpretive park is open from Memorial Day through Labor Day weekend, Tuesday through Sunday from 9 a.m. to 7 p.m. Flush toilets, drinking water, and picnic tables are available. Phone (541) 963-7186 for information.

7. Whitman Mission (Washington)

Missionaries **Marcus and Narcissa Whitman** in 1836 established a mission near today's Walla Walla, Washington, that became a regular stop on the Oregon Trail during the early 1840s. The Whitmans had traveled west with a goal of converting American Indians to the Christian faith. The pair held regular church services, preaching the Bible and singing hymns for the local Cayuse. Communication was a problem since the Whitmans neither learned the Cayuse language and customs nor taught English to the Cayuse.

A view of where Whitman Mission once served as a popular pioneer stop during the early years of the trail.

Dr. Whitman did teach the Cayuse to plant crops such as wheat, corn, and potatoes. Trained as a medical doctor, he also attended to their medical needs. The Cayuse welcomed his help with the sick but worried about what they considered his supernatural powers.

Once the early Oregon Trail wagon trains began arriving, much of the Whitmans' time was spent assisting and trying to convert the pioneers rather than the Cayuse. The increasing numbers of white people passing through also caused the Cayuse to fear that the pioneers would attempt to seize their land.

By the mid-1840s most pioneers used a shorter route south of the Umatilla River that avoided **Whitman Mission.** At this point it was generally only the emigrants who required assistance, were sick, or needed a place to spend the winter who crossed the river to visit the mission. Still distressed by the Whitmans' neglect and the flow of wagon trains crossing their paths, the Cayuse gave Marcus Whitman several warnings that he was no longer welcome. Despite this, the Whitmans remained.

During an outbreak of measles in 1847, Dr. Whitman treated both the Cayuse and the pioneers. Although most pioneers recovered, the disease killed about half the Cayuse tribe. Unfortunately for the missionaries, the Cayuse had a tradition that the family of the person who died had a right to kill the medicine man whose medicines failed to work. With whites recovering and large numbers of their own dying, the Cayuse suspected bad medicine. On November 29, 1847, Marcus and Narcissa Whitman along with eleven others were killed at the mission. About fifty survivors were held captive for a month until ransomed by the Hudson's Bay Company. In 1936, 100 years following its establishment, the Whitman Mission was honored by becoming Whitman Mission National Historic Site.

Whitman Mission is approximately 6 miles west of Walla Walla via US 12. About 5.6 miles west of town, turn south (left) on Sweagle Road and then east (left) on Whitman Mission Road.

8. Lower Umatilla River Crossing

Following the 1847 uprising and resulting deaths at Whitman Mission, travel across the high desert south of the Columbia River became the main route of emigrants on the Oregon Trail. Along the route the 89-mile-long **Umatilla River** (with headwaters in the Blue Mountains) was crossed twice. The Umatilla's Upper Crossing was in present-day Pendleton, while the **Lower Crossing** was in today's small community of Echo, where the emigrants often stopped to camp. The grassy area beside the river offered firewood, plentiful grass for feeding livestock, and clean water for drinking and doing laundry.

By 1851 the west bank of the river sported a white frame building housing the Umatilla Indian Agency, which also served as a trading post and in 1852 added a post office. By 1855 the military stockade of Fort Henrietta had replaced the agency that was burned by the Cayuse earlier in the year. The post was abandoned the following year.

The former pioneer campground is now home to Fort Henrietta Park, a small grassy area beside the river that includes interpretive signs describing the fort and emigrant campground. A small RV park is at the site.

The Lower Crossing is reached by taking exit 188 off I-84 and driving south about a mile to the small community of Echo.

9. Echo Meadows

After crossing the Umatilla River 20-plus miles west of present-day Pendleton, pioneers continued along the Columbia Plateau toward an eventual meeting with the mighty Columbia. By the mid-1840s the trail had shifted away from the Columbia to higher and firmer ground along the Umatilla River. Ahead was a lengthy trip across a largely barren sagebrush-covered landscape.

Echo Meadows has prominent swales across a harsh landscape that remains relatively unchanged since pioneer days.

Four miles west of the Umatilla crossing, excellent swales are evident in **Echo Meadows.** While the swales here were once much more extensive, cultivation in the 1970s left only a 320-acre section that has been saved for exploration by today's travelers.

The property is administered by the Bureau of Land Management, which has constructed a parking area, information pavilion, and paved walking path that leads to a mile-long section of the old trail. The 0.5-mile walking path is wide and flat, and includes benches for visitors who haven't been doing much in the way of exercise. The swale itself is open to hiking, but only to the BLM property line. We have visited Echo Meadows on three occasions, and each time we had the place to ourselves.

To reach the site, drive 6.5 miles west on OR 207 from the small community of Echo and turn north for 0.5 mile on a rough gravel road to the Echo Meadows parking lot.

10. John Day River Crossing

After fording the Umatilla River near the present-day town of Echo, pioneers traveled across 50 miles of dry, hilly scrubland to the **McDonald Crossing of the John Day River.** The crossing was about 20 miles southeast of where the river empties into the Columbia. The path across the high desert south of the Columbia avoided steep

A view down the hill toward the John Day River, whose firm bed with smooth rocks resulted in a relatively easy ford.

canyons and sandy ground that lined the river. The riverbed at McDonald Crossing was firm and lined with smooth river rocks, resulting in a relatively easy ford. A ferry and, later, a bridge were located near the original crossing.

The John Day was named for a member of the American Fur Company's 1810 expedition from Missouri to the mouth of the Columbia River. The river descends nearly 9,000 feet over its 284-mile length from its headwaters. It remains undammed and is one of the longest free-flowing rivers in the continental United States.

The crossing can be approached from either the east or west. We chose the eastern approach, believing the access road to be more suitable for our rental car. From I-84 take exit 129 south and drive 8 miles on Blalock Canyon Road before turning west (right) on Lower Rock Creek Road. Drive about 6 miles to a Y junction and take the right fork to the crossing. The swale of the Oregon Trail as it descends to the crossing is relatively easy to identify. Look for several white trail markers up the hill.

11. Descent to the Columbia River

The **Deschutes River** proved a difficult ford, causing pioneer wagon trains to descend off the tableland in order to cross the river near where it empties into the Columbia. After fording the river, pioneers climbed the hill just beyond the opposite bank and headed for The Dalles, where the overland portion of the trip would end until 1846 with the opening of the Barlow Road.

Pioneers descended this steep grade to reach the south bank of the Columbia River.

The descent of thousands of oxen and wagons created a distinctive and impressive two-track off the plateau that is worthy of inspection. Climbing the two-track to the top where a fence and No Trespassing sign are encountered offers a magnificent view of the Columbia River.

Looking east, this is the steep hill pioneers descended to ford the Deschutes River at the point it empties into the Columbia.

The descent landmark is on the south side of the Biggs Rufus Highway/OR 207, approximately 2 miles west of Biggs Junction. The landmark is easy to miss driving west, and you've gone too far if you arrive at the entrance to the Deschutes River State Recreation Area. Turn around and return east approximately 2.4 miles. A small pull-off for parking is near the base of the two-track.

12. Deschutes River Crossing

Heading west, south of the Columbia River required the emigrants to undertake several river crossings, none more difficult than the mouth of the Deschutes River. The Deschutes flows 252 miles north from its headwaters on the eastern side of the Cascade Range and is a major tributary of the Columbia. John Fremont described the river's mouth as it entered the Columbia as a "roar of falls and rapids." Completion of Dalles Dam in 1957 considerably altered the character of the location where the emigrants crossed.

Emigrants floated their wagons across the river's mouth while livestock were required to swim. If the water level was high, emigrants would make use of an island in the river for the crossing. According to a wooden historical marker at the crossing: "Pioneer women and children were frequently ferried across the stream by Native canoe men who made the passage in exchange for bright colored shirts and other trade goods."

The east side of the river is now occupied by an attractive Oregon state recreation area that offers camping and picnicking. The park offers an interpretive kiosk with information panels about the Oregon Trail.

Deschutes River Crossing is 4.5 miles southwest of Biggs Junction on the Biggs Rufus Highway/OR 206.

The Deschutes River at the location where pioneers forded.

13. Fort Dalles

A volunteer militia in 1848 became the first military unit to occupy an abandoned Methodist mission established at The Dalles 10 years earlier. Two years later the former mission would become a minor military post manned by a small number of US army troops who, along with the assistance of trail emigrants, set about constructing several new buildings. Additional soldiers arrived later that year, and Camp Drum was established to assist and protect emigrants headed to the Willamette Valley. The facility would be expanded and its name changed to **Fort Dalles** in 1853.

During the Yakama Indian Wars of 1855–1856, eight companies of soldiers were assigned to the fort, resulting in the need for several additional buildings including a hospital and guardhouse. Those in charge of the new construction chose German immigrant Louis Scholl's Gothic cottage style, which included bay windows and pointed gables. The finished buildings received mostly negative reviews from US Army brass, in large part because they considered the construction too costly.

With reduced emigrant travel and a decline in conflicts with American Indians, many of the soldiers were reassigned back East following the start of the Civil War in 1861. A decade later the land was transferred to the Department of the Interior. The surviving post's Surgeon's Quarters, built in 1856, was deeded to the Oregon Historical Society in 1903 after the founding members of the society from The Dalles advocated for the historic building's preservation. In 1905 the Surgeon's Quarters opened as the Fort Dalles Museum, one of the state's oldest history museums. Ownership of the Fort Dalles Surgeon's Quarters was transferred in 1953 to the Wasco County–Dalles City Museum Commission. The museum has a varied collection that includes pioneer wagons and old vehicles. It is located at the corner of 500 W. 15th Street and Garrison Street in The Dalles. Phone (541) 296-4547 for information.

14. Fort Vancouver (Washington)

Fort Vancouver was established in 1825 as a fur trading post by the London-based Hudson's Bay Company (HBC) on a bluff above the Columbia River. It was moved a mile west in 1829, primarily for easier access to the river. The fort had a palisade of upright logs approximately 20 feet high. The increasing number of Americans arriving in the area caused the British to construct a bastion on the fort's northwest corner in the 1840s. Within the walls were approximately forty buildings that included offices, living quarters, workshops, a chapel, and a schoolhouse. The center of the fort's life and business was the large two-story house of the chief factor, **Dr. John McLoughlin**.

Under McLoughlin's leadership, the HBC's reach soon covered the entire Northwest, with the fort serving as HBC's Columbia District headquarters. Not only was

The Dalles: Early End of the Oregon Trail

The Dalles, one of Oregon's oldest communities, became a hub of activity in the 1840s as Oregon Trail pioneers arrived during their journey to the Willamette Valley. At the time the ever-dangerous Columbia River surged with a series of treacherous rapids lined by basalt rock. Until 1846, when Sam Barlow opened a route around the south shoulder of Mount Hood, the overland portion of the Oregon Trail effectively ended at The Dalles. Pioneers either abandoned their prairie schooners and most possessions and continued on foot, or disassembled the wagons to be loaded onto rafts for transport downriver. Some newcomers liked the area and chose to remain and make it their home.

Indigenous people had used this area for thousands of years as a place to fish, with annual gatherings during which they traded with other tribes in the spring and fall. Salmon had long served as a dietary staple of American Indians, who continue to hold treaty fishing rights along the Columbia River.

Members of the Lewis and Clark Expedition, among the first white men to visit the area, camped nearby for three nights in 1805 at a site they called "Rock Fort Camp." They chose the same campsite the following year on their return to St. Louis. The site is marked with a National Park Service interpretive sign. Soon fur trappers, traders, and other explorers arrived, followed by missionaries who traveled here to Christianize the area's local Indigenous people. The Wascopam Mission, built by Methodist-Episcopal missionaries Daniel Lee and Henry K. W. Perkins in 1838, is long gone but memorialized by Pulpit Rock, which stands today in the middle of a city street.

The town was incorporated in 1857 as Dalles City, a name changed later to The Dalles. The name originated with French Canadian fur trappers who called this section of the river "Les Grandes Dalles de la Columbia." Their generalized meaning for *dalles* was "rapids of a river through a narrow rock-lined channel."

The Dalles remains an interesting city worthy of a full day's visit. The first territorial courthouse west of the Rocky Mountains was built in 1859 and today is used as a museum. The Columbia Gorge Discovery Center and Museum is the official interpretive center for the Columbia River Gorge National Scenic Area. Fort Dalles, built in 1856, is Oregon's second-oldest history museum. Over seventy of the town's buildings are listed on the National Register of Historic Places. Brochures and walking maps are available from the chamber of commerce at 404 W. 2nd Street.

The End of the Trail marker in The Dalles
End of the Trail Park.

A bastion at the reconstructed Fort Vancouver.

the native Canadian a skillful fur trader, but he appreciated the potential of the rich soil for growing crops and feeding cattle, the river for a supply of salmon and transportation, and the trees as a source of lumber. McLoughlin established farms and orchards, brought in cattle, and built salmon fisheries, grain mills, and sawmills. The resulting products not only supplied the fort's population of 500 to 700 people, but also were internationally exported to offset the decline in the fur trade.

Fort Vancouver had become the hub of Northwest commerce by the 1830s when it exerted a major influence on political and social affairs and served as a major stop for travelers. Dr. Marcus and Narcissa Whitman visited in 1836 to purchase supplies before establishing their mission near today's Walla Walla, Washington. When the westward expansion began in 1842, exhausted pioneers traveling by raft down the Columbia River or overland were often out of supplies and money. At the fort they could acquire needed provisions on credit.

As more and more American settlers claimed land on the south side of the Columbia River, McLoughlin's superiors were concerned they would lose control of that area. The boundary was disputed between the Americans and the British until the 1846 Oregon Treaty was signed. The treaty set the official boundary at the 49th parallel, causing the HBC to move its Columbia District headquarters to Fort Victoria on Vancouver Island while using Fort Vancouver as a trading post. Dr. John McLoughlin took a furlough from HBC in 1846 and moved to Oregon City.

In 1849 the US Army built a post on a rise just above Fort Vancouver. The HBC continued to use the fort until 1860. Once they departed, the army reused some of the trading post's buildings, but in 1866 a fire burned the fort to the ground.

The Fort Vancouver site became a national monument under the National Park Service in 1948. Reconstruction of the fort commenced in the 1960s, and it was designated a national historic site in 1961. Several reconstructed buildings are in place including the chief factor's house, the blacksmith and carpenter shops, the American Indian trade shop, and a hospital. A garden outside the gates is similar to one that furnished food for the chief factor's house.

The reconstructed fort is open Tuesday through Saturday with the exception of major holidays. It is located at 1501 E. Evergreen Boulevard, Vancouver, Washington. Phone (360) 816-6230 or check the fort's website at www.nps.gov/fova for current information.

15. Tygh Valley

Pioneers choosing to follow the **Barlow Road** rather than risk a raft trip down the Columbia faced a difficult trek across mountainous terrain. The travel was hard regardless of whether they departed south from The Dalles or took a more direct route from the east after fording the John Day River.

A westward view of Mount Hood near where pioneers approached Tygh Valley and the Barlow Road.

A view of Mount Hood from Timberline Lodge.

Timberline Lodge: A Treasure of Craftsmanship

Timberline Lodge, perched on the south shoulder of Oregon's Mount Hood at an elevation of 6,000 feet, is an interesting stop for travelers following the trail's Barlow Road alternative in Oregon. Timberline is an extraordinary facility worthy of comparison with Yellowstone National Park's Old Faithful Inn, Yosemite's Ahwahnee, and Glacier's Many Glacier Hotel for both its history and its splendor.

Timberline was constructed during 1936–1937 as a Federal Arts Project under the Works Progress Administration (WPA), a program initiated by President Franklin Roosevelt to put unemployed Americans back to work. Almost 500 male and female employees with an average age of 55 were hired and paid a fair salary for their work on the lodge.

The art program allowed workers to learn a trade by training with skilled artists and craftspeople. A master blacksmith taught workers to craft hand-wrought furniture, decorative gates, unusual light fixtures, and attractive door hinges and handles. Craftspeople created murals and carved newel posts from recycled utility poles. Weavers wove fabric for drapes and upholstery; rugs were hooked by hand, and curtains and bedspreads in guest rooms were appliquéd. Art also included oil paintings, watercolors, glass murals, and more. The entire building is a treasure of craftsmanship.

Today most artwork remains in its original location. Drapes and upholstery have been replaced, but, like the originals, with hand-woven fabrics created by local craftspeople.

It's best to spend the night, but even travelers without an extra night to spend here should at least stop for a couple of hours to admire Timberline's exterior and explore the lobby and mezzanine. The lodge was built long after the Oregon Trail had gone dormant, but the opportunity to visit this wonderful building and admire the craftsmanship of its builders is well worth the time.

Timberline Lodge is approximately 6 miles northeast of US 26 at Government Camp. It is an hour and a half west of Portland.

Both trails led to the scenic **Tygh Valley** on the eastern side of the Cascade Range. This small, fertile valley, named for the Tygh tribe that inhabited the area, offered a pleasant resting place where the emigrants prepared for the demanding climb over the Cascade Mountains. During their stop, the pioneers often traded with the local tribe or purchased needed supplies at a trading post operated by a Frenchman.

Tygh Valley is 30 miles south of The Dalles via US 197. To access the town, turn right on Tygh Valley Road at the bottom of the hill. This road heads toward Wamic and parallels much of the Barlow Road.

16. Barlow Pass

The **Barlow Road** reached an elevation of 4,157 feet at the point where it crossed over the Cascade Range. Today the Oregon Department of Transportation marks the pass on OR 35 at 4,161 feet. The old **Barlow Pass** is just south of OR 35 on FR 3530. The well-marked road also leads to the Pacific Crest Trail and a Sno-Park. A parking area is near the Forest Service's impressive Barlow Road sign, which was carved in the 1930s by a forest ranger.

Barlow Pass now serves as a trailhead for an 8.8-mile path that follows a portion of the old Barlow Road. A snowshoeing trail also begins at the trailhead but

A sign at the Barlow Road summit indicates pioneers had traveled 1,947 miles from Independence, with 54 miles remaining to Oregon City.

eventually branches off from the hiking trail. If the weather is pleasant, consider walking a portion of the Barlow Road to enjoy the silence of the beautiful forest. During the walk imagine being accompanied by pioneer wagons along with weary but joyous emigrants who were nearing their destination.

17. Pioneer Woman's Grave

The original grave of a female pioneer was uncovered in 1924 during construction of the Mount Hood Loop Highway when workers clearing an overgrown area discovered a wagon-box casket. The remains were reburied beside the highway with stones and a wooden cross placed atop the grave.

A number of markers have adorned the gravesite over the years. The site's current bronze plaque was dedicated in 1982 by the Multnomah Chapter of the Daughters of the American Revolution. It begins: "In Memory of an Unknown Pioneer Woman of 184?."

An interpretive display by the Mount Hood National Forest explains how the grave was discovered. It also includes a story from the son of the Barlow Road

The grave of an unknown pioneer woman is near the Barlow Road, a short distance off OR 35.

tollgate superintendent, who says he remembers his father telling him that a man with a young girl and boy had just buried his wife in a wagon box by the road. Over the years numerous items including flowers, stuffed animals, and coins have been placed on the stones of the grave.

From OR 35 turn south on FR 3531, approximately 2 miles west of Barlow Pass. Drive 0.75 mile; the gravesite is on the right atop a small rise.

18. Laurel Hill Chute

Sam Barlow's road through the forest to Oregon City may have offered a safer route than challenging the rapids of the Columbia in rafts, but it certainly wasn't an easy trip. One of the most forbidding obstacles proved to be **Laurel Hill,** an exceedingly steep downward gradient off the south slope of Mount Hood. Considered by many as the most difficult descent along the entire trail, the chute required that emigrants slowly lower their wagons with ropes wrapped around trees. The Barlow Road was eventually realigned to bypass Laurel Hill.

A hiking trail to the chute begins beside a small parking area between mileposts 50 and 51 on US 26. The pull-off is accessible only from the eastbound lane of the divided highway. The rocky chute may be observed from the bottom after climbing about sixty

The view looking down from the top of the Laurel Hill Chute, which proved one of the most challenging obstacles of the Barlow Road.

steps to an old, abandoned roadbed. A hiking trail with numerous switchbacks leads to a higher elevation and a view of the chute from the top.

19. Barlow Road Tollgate

Sam Barlow and partner **Philip Foster** finished clearing a pioneer wagon path skirting the south shoulder of Mount Hood in 1846. The 80-mile toll road connecting The Dalles, Tygh Valley, and Eagle Creek allowed emigrants to avoid rafting down the dangerous Columbia River, but at a price. The charge was $5 per wagon plus 10 cents per head of livestock. Barlow terminated his partnership with Foster at the expiration of his concession in 1848.

The road continued with Barlow's name while the concession changed owners several times over nearly 60 years of operation. The tollgate moved four times, each succeeding gate being farther west. The fifth and final tollgate was established in 1879 near the present-day community of Rhododendron. The location was on a narrow terrace that made it difficult for travelers to bypass and avoid paying a toll. A replica gate has been placed at the site that once had three structures including a log house. Two large maples, one on each side of the gate, were planted by the tollgate operator in the late 1800s, which made it possible for historians to determine the location of the fifth tollgate. One of the trees was diseased and cut in 2019.

Despite the seemingly high toll charged to the pioneers, the road required continuous maintenance and proved generally unprofitable. In part this was due to many pioneers having little money remaining by the time they had reached this point. According to the application for the National Register of Historic places, books maintained at the fifth tollgate included this entry for July 18, 1897:

> Wm. Russell & family W(est) 2 team(s) & 2 Wagons going to Tillamock but little money had to take a lot of store goods as pay & no extra cash. Took all he had good for anything. Cash I tried to get, half cash. Vowed he could not pay any.
>
> | | |
> |---|---|
> | 2 prs. Suspenders | 60 |
> | 6 Hankerchiefs | 50 |
> | 7 prs. Hose | 70 |
> | 9 prs. Half Hose | 75 |
> | 2 cards Buttons | 23 |
> | 3 cards Needles | 15 |
> | 1 prs. Suspenders | 35 |
> | | $3.28 |

The tollgate is a short distance southeast of Rhododendron on US 26 between mileposts 44 and 45. It is on the south side of the road and includes a small parking area.

20. Philip Foster Farm

The farm of **Philip Foster** was the last major stop along the **Barlow Road** before emigrants arrived in the Willamette Valley. Foster established a store on the farm that offered fresh vegetables and meat, along with hay for livestock. He also built several cabins available for short stays.

Sam Barlow and His Overland Road to the Willamette Valley

Sam Barlow was born in Kentucky in 1795 and later resided in Indiana and Illinois before heading west in 1845 with his wife, six children, and multiple wagons. A September arrival in The Dalles, where the overland portion of the Oregon Trail then terminated, encountered a crowd of emigrants seeking transportation down the Columbia River to Fort Vancouver. Discouraged by the wait and cost of having the wagons transported by rafts on the dangerous river, Barlow headed south in an effort to discover an overland route to the Willamette Valley.

Barlow, along with several companions, scouted ahead of the main group and learned of an American Indian trail that skirted the southern base of Mount Hood. Returning to the group, the men discovered another larger wagon train hoping to join the search for an overland route. The combined group then returned to the forest and commenced the hard work of cutting and burning to clear a trail for the wagons.

Being late in the year, the pioneers became concerned about the coming winter and made the decision to leave the wagons and supplies in the hands of a guard while setting out with a packtrain for Oregon City, which was destined to become the territory's first capital. In Oregon City Barlow convinced the state's provisional legislature to charter a toll road for the route he planned. Organizing a partnership, he raised money and hired over three dozen men to build the 80-mile road that opened to pioneers in 1846.

Although the Mount Hood Road (most emigrants called it the **Barlow Road**) attracted considerable traffic, it proved unprofitable and the partners threw in the towel after 2 years. A series of owners followed until in 1919 the road was gifted by its owners to the state of Oregon.

Portions of the original Barlow Road can still be driven, although some sections are winding and considered dangerous. Today's travelers uninterested in driving on the old road can enjoy some beautiful scenery by hiking portions of the road. A paved road parallels much of the old road that was built nearly 200 years ago by a Kentuckian headed to a new life in Oregon Territory.

In 1843 Foster and his family arrived by boat in Oregon City where he and a brother-in-law established a general store. During the same year he staked a claim to 640 acres of land in today's town of Eagle Creek. Here he built a log cabin and commenced farming.

In 1845 Foster and his two sons connected with emigrant Sam Barlow, who was attempting to blaze a new trail to the Willamette Valley that would allow pioneers to avoid the dangerous and expensive raft trip down the Columbia River. Foster and his sons assisted Barlow in selecting a route and clearing the trail that became a toll road known as the Barlow Road. The majority of emigrants chose to travel along the new road, and Foster's farm served as a popular stop where the pioneers rested, sometimes for several days, while allowing their livestock to graze.

The farm is now operated by a historical society that offers tours. The original home burned in 1880, and the family home currently on the farm was constructed in 1883. The oldest remaining building is the barn that was built in 1874. A replica of

The Phillip Foster Farm and store was one of the last stops for pioneers traveling the Barlow Road.

Foster's original store is stocked with items from the 1800s and early 1900s, along with handcrafted products such as candles and ironwork. The grounds are open daily from dawn to dusk. Tours (fee charged) are offered Monday, Wednesday, and Saturday from 11 a.m. to 4 p.m.

The farm is located at 22725 SE Eagle Creek Road in Eagle Creek. It is about 16 miles east of Oregon City, just east of the junction of OR 224 and OR 211. Call (503) 637-6324 for information.

21. Home of John McLoughlin

Due in part to the assistance he offered American and foreign emigrants to the Northwest, Canadian **John McLoughlin** took a leave of absence from the London-based Hudson's Bay Company in 1846 following 20 years as chief factor of **Fort Vancouver**. This same year he moved into a house he had built on land near Willamette Falls. McLoughlin became an American citizen in 1851, which helped ensure his claim to the land that in 1846 had become part of the United States' Oregon Territory.

Although not fancy by today's standards, McLoughlin's home was built of finished lumber and considered luxurious at a time when most of the area's population lived in log cabins. The two-story house includes four second-story bedrooms plus a large parlor, office, sewing room, and dining room on the first floor. McLoughlin lived in the

Dr. John McLoughlin, Canadian Friend of the Pioneers

John McLoughlin's large stature referred not only to his six-foot, four-inch height, but also his leadership as chief factor at Fort Vancouver, a trading post frequented by early pioneers nearing the end of their journey on the Oregon Trail. Born in Canada, McLoughlin trained to become a physician, although his first job with the North West Company allowed him to work as a doctor only during summers. The remainder of the year he served as a clerk who proved to be an excellent trader.

McLoughlin continued working on the business side of the North West Company, which merged in 1821 with the Hudson's Bay Company. By that time McLoughlin had worked his way up to become chief factor, or leader, of a post on the Canadian border with present-day Minnesota. In 1824 he was transferred to the Columbia District, a huge area that ranged from the crest of the Rocky Mountains to the Pacific Ocean, north to Alaska, and south into California.

Dr. John McLoughlin as chief factor of Fort Vancouver was a friend of the pioneers. PUBLIC DOMAIN

The Canadian was given wide authority to make decisions for what to that point had been an unprofitable business, and make them he did. Headquarters was moved from Fort Astoria to Fort Vancouver, fur trapping became more organized, crops were planted, a lumber mill was added, and salmon were caught and dried. McLoughlin utilized these and other products to develop and manage what became an international trading network.

When the stream of emigrants began arriving in the early 1840s, McLoughlin was generous with help by extending credit to pioneers who were exhausted and mostly broke. This and a decline in business brought disagreements with his supervisor, and in 1845 the company divided his district into several smaller units while reducing his pay and authority. This caused McLaughlin to request a leave of absence in 1846 that lasted until mid-1849, when he retired.

McLoughlin built a house in Oregon City where he owned a mercantile store and was involved with milling interests. He became a US citizen in 1851 and died at his home in 1857. McLoughlin's home is now a unit of the National Park Service's Fort Vancouver National Historic Site and open to visitors.

The home of Fort Vancouver chief factor John McLoughlin in Oregon City is part of Fort Vancouver National Historic Site.

home from 1846 until his death in 1857. His wife, Marguerite, continued living in the home with daughter Eloisa and her family until Marguerite's death in 1860.

The **McLoughlin House,** a unit of Fort Vancouver National Historic Site, was moved in 1909 from its original location near the falls to higher ground. The home has been restored to the period when the John McLoughlin family resided here. The graves of McLoughlin and Marguerite are next to the home. The McLoughlin House is located in Oregon City at 713 Center Street, and is part of a local historic district. Tour information is available next door in the Barclay House, which was once the home of a Hudson's Bay Company associate. Call (503) 656-5151 for information about hours of visitation.

INTERPRETIVE CENTERS, MUSEUMS, AND RESOURCES ALONG THE TRAIL

Missouri

Missouri Division of Tourism, visitmo.com, (573) 751-4133

Independence, visitindependence.com, (800) 748-7323

Kansas City, visitkc.com, (800) 767-7700

National Frontier Trails Museum, 318 W. Pacific, Independence, MO 64050, (816) 325-7575, www.ci.independence.mo.us/NFTM. Includes exhibits on the history of the pioneer trails, with a concentration on the Santa Fe, Oregon, and California Trails that in the early years departed from Independence. America's westward expansion is the theme of a seventeen-minute film. The museum includes a research library and is within walking distance of Independence Courthouse Square, where pioneers and freighters began their journeys. The Oregon-California Trails Association is located next door to the museum.

Kansas

Kansas Travel and Tourism, travelks.com, (785) 296-2009

Lawrence, explorelawrence.com, (785) 856-3040

Topeka, visittopeka.com, (800) 235-1030

Shawnee Indian Mission State Historic Site, 3403 W. 53rd St., Fairway, KS 66205, (913) 262-0867, www.kshs.org/shawnee_indian. One of the three buildings houses exhibits related to the missionaries, American Indians, and overland trails. The mission was a boarding school for American Indian boys and girls from 1839 to 1862.

Kansas Museum of History, 6425 SW 6th Ave., Topeka, KS 66615, (785) 272-8681, www.kshs.org/p/kansas-museum-of-history/19578. The state historical museum presents Kansas history from prehistoric to recent times and includes exhibits on the Santa Fe and Oregon-California Trails. One building from the Potawatomi Baptist Mission, a boarding school for Potawatomi children from 1848 to 1861, is located on the front campus of the museum.

Nebraska

Nebraska Tourism, visitnebraska.org, (402) 471-3796

Gage County Tourism (Beatrice), visitbeatrice.com, (402) 205-3292

Gering, visitgering.com, (308) 436-6888

Jefferson County Visitors Committee (Fairbury), visitoregontrail.org, (402) 729-3000

Kearney, visitkearney.org, (308) 237-3178

Keith County Chamber of Commerce (Ogallala), explorekeithcounty.org/tourism, (308) 204-4066

North Platte Visitors Center, visitnorthplatte.com, (308) 532-4729

Scotts Bluff, visitscottsbluff.com, (800) 788-9475

Rock Creek Station State Historical Park, 57426 CR 710, Fairbury, NE 68352, (402) 729-5777, outdoornebraska.gov/rockcreekstation. The park's relatively small visitor center includes a museum that interprets the colorful history of this scenic trail landmark. Artifacts excavated from the site are on display.

Fort Kearny State Historical Park, 1020 V Rd., Kearney, NE 68845, (308) 865-5305, outdoornebraska.gov/fortkearny. The interpretive center offers exhibits on the fort's history and the soldiers who were stationed here to offer protection for emigrants traveling the Oregon-California Trail. The park includes a replica stockade and blacksmith/carpenter shop. An 18-minute video is shown in a small theater. Living history programs are sometimes offered.

The Archway, 3060 E. 1st St. (I-80, Exit 275), Kearney, NE 68847, (308) 237-1000, archway.org. This unique museum spans I-80, making it difficult to miss. Visitors walk through history and listen to stories, starting with the emigrants who traveled the Oregon Trail to those who followed to travel and live along the Great Platte River Road.

Lincoln County Historical Museum, 2403 N. Buffalo Bill Ave., North Platte, NE 69101, (308) 534-5640, lincolncountymuseum.org. This interesting local museum is composed of a main museum building amid a village of historic structures from the area. Trail exhibits include a trail marker and information on Fort McPherson.

Ash Hollow State Historical Park, P.O. Box 70, US Hwy. 26, Lewellen, NE 69147, (308)778-5651, outdoornebraska.gov/ashhollow. The small visitor center on a bluff overlooking the historic trail has exhibits on American Indians, pioneers, and the geology and paleontology of the park.

Legacy of the Plains Museum, 2930 Old Oregon Trail, Gering, NE 69341, (308) 436-1989, legacyoftheplains.org. The large museum covers 2,000 years of life in the Platte River Valley. A wide variety of items are on display including many from the period of the westward migration. Subjects include transportation, farming, ranching, and more.

Scotts Bluff National Monument, 190276 Old Oregon Trail, Gering, NE 69341, (308) 436-9700, nps.gov/scbl. The visitor center has a museum that covers American Indians, traders, and the emigrants who traveled through the area plus an introductory film. The national monument owns a large collection of William Henry Jackson's original Western artwork, with several reproductions on display.

Wyoming

Wyoming Tourism, travelwyoming.com, (800) 225-5996

Casper, visitcasper.com, (307) 234-5362

Guernsey, townofguernseywy.us/services/visitor_center, (307) 836-2335

Lander Chamber of Commerce Visitor Center, landerchamber.org, (307) 332-3892

Rock Springs and Green River Visitor Center, tourwyoming,com/travel-tools/visitor -center, (307) 382-2538

Fort Laramie National Historic Site, 965 Grey Rocks Rd., Fort Laramie, WY 82212, (307) 837-2221, nps.gov/fola. The National Park Service site is home to a small museum in the visitor center. Several of the restored buildings are furnished in the 1850s–1860s style, including officers' homes, a store, and a barracks with uniforms hanging by the beds.

Wyoming Pioneer Memorial Museum, 400 W. Center St., Douglas, WY 82633, (307) 358-9288, wyoparks.wyo.gov/index.php/places-to-go/Wyoming-pioneer-museum. The museum includes early history of the area with displays of Indigenous and pioneer artifacts and an exhibit on the trails.

National Historic Trails Interpretive Center, 1501 N. Poplar St., Casper, WY 82601, (307) 261-7700, nhtcf.org. An impressive historic trails interpretive center with displays intended to transport visitors to being among pioneers traveling the trails. An excellent 17-minute video presentation, "Footsteps to the West," uses five screens and illuminated dioramas positioned around the room. Several hands-on exhibits include experiencing the pulling/pushing of a Mormon handcart.

Fort Caspar Museum, 4001 Fort Caspar Rd., Casper, WY 82604, (307) 235-8462, fortcasparwyoming.com. The museum offers a look at regional history from prehistoric peoples to the present, with areas devoted to the pioneer trails and the frontier army. Buildings of the reconstructed fort are furnished in an 1865 period style. Replicas of the Mormon Ferry and one section of the Guinard Bridge are also on the property.

Martin's Cove: Mormon Trail Site, 47600 W. Hwy. 220, Alcova, WY 82620, (307) 328-2953, churchofjesuschrist.org/learn/historic-sites/Wyoming/martins-cove?lang=eng. The visitor center has exhibits with artifacts of the Latter-day Saint migration west and the rescue of the Willie and Martin handcart companies in 1856.

Fort Bridger State Historic Site, 37000 I-80 BL, Fort Bridger, WY 82933, (307) 782-3842, wyoparks.wyo.gov/index.php/places-to-go/fort-bridger. Fort Bridger has building replicas covering five eras of occupation including the period in which pioneers passed through on the Oregon, California, and Mormon Trails. The site has a museum with displays and artifacts from one of the historic trail's most noted pioneer stops.

Idaho

Idaho Tourism, visitidaho.org, (800) 847-4843

Montpelier, bearlake.org/loc/Montpelier, (800) 448-2327

Soda Springs, sodaspringsid.com/visitors/

Pocatello, visitpocatello.com, (208) 479-7659

Twin Falls, visitsouthidaho.com, (208) 732-5569

Boise, boise.org, (800) 635-5240

The National Oregon/California Trail Center, 320 N. 4th St., Montpelier, ID 83254, (866) 847-3800, oregontrailcenter.org. Live actors take visitors on a simulated wagon train heading to Oregon. Visitors select supplies and gather around an evening campfire to listen to trail stories told by a wagon master. Paintings, artifacts, and exhibits help tell the story of the trail's history. The trail center includes a re-created mercantile store and gun shop.

Fort Hall Commemorative Trading Post, 3002 Avenue of the Chiefs, Pocatallo, ID 83204, (208) 234-1795, forthall.net. The Bannock County Historical Museum, with exhibits on the Shoshone and Bannock, is next door to the replica of Fort Hall, one of the trail's famous landmarks. The museum offers a history of the early trappers and the great migration west.

Massacre Rocks State Park, 3592 N. Park Ln., American Falls, ID 83211, (208) 548-2672, parksandrecreation.idaho.gov/parks/massacre-rocks. The visitor center contains exhibits on the Oregon Trail and the emigrant–American Indian skirmishes that took place in the area.

Three Island Crossing State Park, 1083 S. Three Island Park Dr., Glenns Ferry, ID 83623, (208) 366-2394, parksandrecreation.idaho.gov/parks/three-island-crossing. The Oregon Trail History and Education Center has exhibits on the trail while highlighting the trail crossing of the three islands. A walking path leads to the location where the wagons emerged on the north bank.

Idaho State Historical Museum, 610 Julia Davis Dr., Boise, ID 83702, (208) 334-2120, history.idaho.gov/museum. Exhibits tell the story of Idaho history including the period pioneers traveled through the area on the Oregon and California Trails. The museum has rotating, permanent, and special exhibits. A Pioneer Village is located beside the museum.

Oregon

Oregon Tourism, traveloregon.com, (800) 547-7842

Baker City, visitBaker.com, (541) 523-5855

Government Camp, mounthoodinfo.com

Oregon City, orcity.org/community/visitor-information, (503) 657-0891

Pendleton, travelpendleton.com, (541) 276-7411

Portland, travelportland.com

Travel Oregon (La Grande), traveloregon.com/places-to-go/cities/la-grande/

Travel Oregon (The Dalles), traveloregon.com/plan-your-trip/oregon-welcome-centers/the-dalles-visitor-center/

National Historic Oregon Trail Interpretive Center, 22267 OR 86, Baker City, OR 97814, (541) 523-1843, blm.gov/learn/interpretive-centers/national-historic-oregon-trail-interpretive-center. A world-class interpretive center atop Flagstaff Hill offers exhibits, films, presentations, and excellent views of the historic trail as it winds into Baker Valley. The facility closed in 2021 for renovation and anticipates reopening for the 2024 season with new exhibits.

Fort Dalles Museum and Anderson Homestead, 500 W. 15th St. and Garrison St., The Dalles, OR 97058, (541) 296-4547, fortdallesmuseum.org. The grounds are home to several buildings including the last remaining structure of Fort Dalles, the 1856 Surgeon's Quarters in which the museum is housed.

Columbia Gorge Discovery Center and Museum, 5000 Discovery Dr., The Dalles, OR 97058, (541) 296-8600, gorgediscovery.org. A major museum with interactive exhibits that trace the history of the Columbia River Gorge, including the area's early explorers. Exhibits include a life-size raft carrying a covered wagon along the rapid current of the Columbia River.

Fort Vancouver National Historic Site, 1501 E. Evergreen Blvd., Vancouver, WA 98661, (360) 816-6230, nps.gov/fova. The reconstructed fort itself is a museum furnished in the style of the 1800s. The visitor center has exhibits and offers a short film about the site's history. The fort was one of the most important stops for many Oregon Trail pioneers.

Mt. Hood Cultural Center and Museum, 88900 Government Camp Loop, Government Camp, OR 97028, (503) 272-3301, mthoodmuseum.org. The museum collection focuses on Mount Hood and the history of the Barlow Road, which passed through what is now Government Camp.

End of the Oregon Trail Interpretive Center, 1726 Washington St., Oregon City, OR 97045, (503) 657-9336, historicoregoncity.org. Everything in this large interpretive center, including films, numerous displays, and visitor activities, is related to the Oregon Trail.

BIBLIOGRAPHY

The books noted below provide good preparation for a trip following the Oregon Trail. Read the books by Dary, Mattes, and Unrah before departing. Become familiar with the Franzwa book and maps, and take both with you. Likewise, the listing and brief descriptions of landmarks along the trail make the Haines book a major asset to carry along.

Dary, David. *The Oregon Trail: An American Saga*. Oxford, NY: Oxford University Press, 2004. An excellent analysis of Oregon Trail history beginning with early exploration of the Northwest and ending with the trail's decline following completion of the transcontinental railroad. Excellent maps, illustrations, and numerous quotes from pioneer journals.

Franzwa, Gregory M. *Maps of the Oregon Trail*. Gerald, MO: The Patrice Press. A valuable reference to take along on a road trip following the trail. An amazing set of maps illustrate the trail's routes and note important landmarks from Independence to Oregon City. Long out of print, but used copies are available from online sellers.

———. *The Oregon Trail Revisited, Silver Anniversary Edition*. Tucson, AZ: The Patrice Press, 1997. This is the bible for travelers intent on exploring every nook and cranny of the trail. Every gravel road, dirt road, two track, and highway that brings a traveler closer to the historic trail is included. With interesting tidbits about people and places, the content offers more than whether to turn left or right. Pack this book along on the trip.

Haines, Aubrey L. *Historic Sites along the Oregon Trail*. Tucson, AZ: The Patrice Press, 1994. An excellent companion for an Oregon Trail road trip with summaries of approximately 400 sites along the route. Images and limited maps are included.

Mattes, Merrill J. *The Great Platte River Road: The Covered Wagon Mainline via Fort Kearny to Fort Laramie*. Lincoln: University of Nebraska Press, 1969; Bison Books printing 1987. Although limited to pioneer travel along Nebraska's Platte River Valley, Mattes offers a concise and interesting history of the emigrant experience during the first third of the journey to Oregon.

National Park Service, National Trails System–Intermountain Region. *National Historic Trails: Auto Tour Route Interpretive Guides, 2005–06*. The National Park Service publishes and distributes four free guides, each covering a different state. Unfortunately, the NPS must have depleted its financial resources before publishing a guide for Oregon. Each guide includes trail history and a short description and access information for numerous sites and interpretive centers. The guides are typically available without charge at visitor centers and interpretive centers along the way. The National Park Service internet site for information on the Oregon Trail is www.nps.gov/oreg.

Unruh, John D. Jr. *The Plains Across: The Overland Emigrants and the Trans-Mississippi West, 1840–1860*. Urbana and Chicago: University of Illinois Press, 1979. An award-winning book some critics call the best book written about the country's westward expansion. Rather than a chronological history, Unruh develops trail history in terms of various factors such as government policy, emigrant–American Indian relations, and business enterprises that influenced travel on the trail.

IMPORTANT DATES ON THE OREGON TRAIL

1792—The *Columbia*, sailing from Boston under Captain Robert Gray, discovers the mouth of a river along the northwest coast. He names the river after his ship.

1803—Under President Thomas Jefferson's leadership, the United States completes the Louisiana Purchase from France for $15 million.

1804—The Lewis and Clark Expedition is dispatched by President Thomas Jefferson to discover a water route to the West Coast.

1810—John Jacob Astor sends a group of men by ship to establish a trading post at the mouth of the Columbia River near present-day Astoria. A second group was sent overland from St. Louis the following year.

1812—Working for John Jacob Astor, John Stuart leads a group of six men eastbound from their trading post on the West Coast. Following directions of an American Indian they will find a break in the Rocky Mountains now known as South Pass. Their discovery of an easy route over the Continental Divide did not receive much public attention due to the War of 1812.

1823–1824—William Ashley hires one hundred men to accompany him to the West and work as fur trappers. Among the men are Jim Bridger, Jedediah Smith, Kit Carson, and Jim Beckwourth. The group rediscovers South Pass.

1830—Jedediah Smith, David E. Jackson, and William Sublette lead ten wagons across the Rocky Mountains at South Pass to a rendezvous on the Wind River.

1832—Benjamin Bonneville departs Missouri with twenty ox-drawn wagons that would cross South Pass along what would become the Oregon Trail.

1834—Nathaniel Wyeth and William Sublette lead a group to a rendezvous on the Green River. With them is Reverend Jason Lee, one of the first missionaries to go west.

William Sublette and Robert Campbell establish Fort William, a trading post that eventually becomes the location of Fort Laramie.

Nathaniel Wyeth establishes Fort Hall, which he eventually sells to the Hudson's Bay Company.

1836—Dr. Marcus and Narcissa Whitman and Reverend Henry and Eliza Spalding travel overland to present-day Washington to establish missions and forcibly Christianize American Indians. The two women are the first known white women to cross the Continental Divide at South Pass.

1841—The Bidwell-Bartleson Party, consisting of about sixty pioneers, heads to California under the leadership of mountain man Thomas Fitzpatrick. The group divides at present-day Soda Springs, Idaho, with about half heading to California and most of the others to Oregon. Father Pierre-Jean De Smet, a Jesuit priest, splits off at Fort Hall to establish his first mission in the West near present-day Missoula, Montana.

1842—The Army Topographical Corps sends a team to explore and map the Oregon Trail to the Rocky Mountains. The team is led by Lieutenant John C. Fremont and guided by Kit Carson.

1843—The Great Migration begins. Approximately 900 people with 100 wagons leave Missouri for the Willamette Valley in present-day Oregon.

The provisional government in Oregon allows land claims to be filed in Oregon City. Married couples could file on up to 640 acres at no cost.

A second expedition of John C. Fremont's group, guided by Kit Carson, covers more of the Oregon Trail and the West including parts of California.

Jim Bridger and Louis Vasquez establish the trading post of Fort Bridger on the Green River.

1844—John C. Fremont's published report of his 1843 expedition, including the excellent maps drawn by Charles Preuss, becomes a travel guide and an inspiration for many to head west.

1846—Sam Barlow and others complete a toll road around the south shoulder of Mount Hood.

The United States and Britain agree to the 49th parallel as the northern border for the Oregon Territory.

The Donner Party is trapped by a winter snowstorm in the Sierra Nevada. Surviving members are driven to cannibalism.

1847—Dr. Marcus and Narcissa Whitman and eleven others are killed at their mission by the Cayuse.

1848—The cholera epidemic strikes Independence, Missouri.

Fort Kearny is established on the Great Platte River Road as the first military post to protect travelers on the Oregon Trail.

Oregon country becomes an official territory of the United States.

Gold is discovered in California.

1849—Thousands of gold-seekers hit the trail to California.

The cholera epidemic spreads as far west as Fort Laramie.

1850—An increasing number of pioneers hit the trail with thousands dying of cholera.

California becomes a state.

A new land law goes into effect. The Donation Land Act allows white settlers and "American half-breed Indians" over 18 years old to file for unclaimed free land; if single they receive 320 acres and if married, 640 acres. They are required to live on and farm the land for 4 years. Settlers arriving after 1850 are entitled to only half the original amount.

1851—The US government meets with representatives of most of the Plains Indian tribes hoping to ensure peace. They sign the Fort Laramie Treaty of 1851, also known as the Horse Creek Treaty.

Travel on the Oregon Trail decreases significantly due to the cholera epidemic.

1854—The Grattan Massacre occurs east of Fort Laramie. Due to a misunderstanding, twenty-nine soldiers, including Lieutenant John Grattan, are killed by Lakota Sioux. The result is the beginning of the Plains Indian Wars.

1858—Gold is discovered in Colorado.

1859—The Leavenworth and Pikes Peak Express becomes one of the first stagecoach lines transporting passengers and mail along the Oregon Trail.

Oregon becomes a state.

1860—The Pony Express begins carrying mail from St. Joseph, Missouri, to Sacramento, California.

1861—Following Western Union's completion of the transcontinental telegraph line, the Pony Express folds after 18 months in service.

The Civil War begins. Troops are removed from frontier posts to help fight in the war.

1862—The Homestead Act is passed by Congress. The act gives an adult citizen, or intended citizen, 160 acres of unclaimed public land for free if they build a home and farm the property for 5 years.

1863—Gold is discovered in Montana.

1869—The transcontinental railroad is completed.

Some still traveled by wagon train through the 1880s. Ezra Meeker, in 1906, was the last known person to travel by wagon on the Oregon Trail.

INDEX

ACKNOWLEDGMENTS

Road trips offer a variety of personal rewards, one of the most valuable being inter-actions with new and interesting people. This has proved true during each of our own journeys, including the latest Oregon Trail trip. From volunteers in small muse-ums to national and state park personnel, we came across numerous individuals with a shared interest in the historic trails and their preservation. Many we met in person during the trip, while others were contacted while gathering information prior to departure or following our return home.

Our 2021 Oregon Trail journey started with a visit to the Oregon-California Trail Association headquarters in Independence, Missouri, where longtime manager Kathy Conway talked with us about the organization, its upcoming annual convention, and several members we might want to contact. The latter proved valuable advice, and we later benefited from conversations and emails with the organization's president, John Briggs.

Jason Vlcan and Scott Stadler of the Bureau of Land Management were particu-larly helpful with photos and offering advice along with directions during our travel through Wyoming. Eric Grunwald at Scotts Bluff National Monument and Michelle Bahe of the Fort Caspar Museum assisted with the William Henry Jackson images at the beginning of each chapter, in addition to offering suggestions for some of our landmark narratives. Susan Buce of the Columbia Gorge Discovery Center and Museum introduced us to the rich history of The Dalles. Megan Huff, curator at Fort Vancouver National Historic Site, provided help with information about the fort and its chief factor, John McLoughlin.

Along the Great Platte River Road we received assistance from Nebraska State Historical Park superintendents including Michaela Clemmons at Rock Creek Station, Eugene Hunt at Fort Kearny, and Tamara Cooper at Ash Hollow. Clayton Hanson helped with Fort Laramie National Historic Site. Likewise, we owe thanks to Jennifer Laughlin at Shawnee Mission in Kansas, Leigh Elmore of the Rice-Tremonti Home in Missouri, Jim Kirkland at Three Island Crossing State Park in Idaho, and Galen Wilson in Idaho's unique community of Soda Springs.

Above all, our thanks to Globe Pequot editor Amy Lyons and her assistant Greta Schmitz for all they have done to turn our initial proposal into something we hope you will find enjoyable and helpful.

Kay and David Scott
Valdosta, Georgia
April 2022

ABOUT THE AUTHORS

Authors Kay and David Scott at California Hill in western Nebraska.

Kay Woelfel Scott was born in Austin, Minnesota, and raised in Yankton, South Dakota, and Clearwater, Florida. She earned degrees from Florida Southern College and the University of Arkansas. **David Scott** was born and raised in Rushville, Indiana. He graduated from Purdue University, Florida State University, and earned a PhD in economics from the University of Arkansas.

Travel and writing about their adventures have been a major part of their lives. They have authored a weekly travel column for a national newspaper chain and discussed travel as guests on NBC's *Today* and numerous radio shows. They have authored three national park guides in addition to *The Complete Guide to the National Park Lodges*, which is currently in its ninth edition. David is also the author of over two dozen business books including *Wall Street Words* and *The American Heritage Dictionary of Business Terms*.

David and Kay Scott live in Valdosta, Georgia. Visit their website at blog.valdost .edu/dlscott.